The Te   eries

The ELT Manager's Handbook

*Practical advice on managing
a successful language school*

Graham Impey
Nic Underhill

**MACMILLAN
HEINEMANN**
English Language Teaching

Macmillan Education

Between Towns Road, Oxford OX4 3PP,UK

A division of Macmillan Publishers Limited

Companies and representatives throughout the world

Heinemann is a registered trademark of Reed Educational & Professional Publishing Limited

ISBN 0 435 24090 0

Series design by Mike Brain

Cover photos by Paul Freestone, Brighton Borough Council,
Ace Photo Agency (background)

Illustrated by: Michael Parsons

Printed in Thailand

2008 2007 2006 2005 2004 2003
16 15 14 13 12 11 10 9 8 7 6

Contents

The Teacher Development Series

TEACHER DEVELOPMENT is the process of becoming the best teacher you can be. It means becoming a student of learning, your own as well as that of others. It represents a widening of the focus of teaching to include not only the subject matter and the teaching methods, but also the people who are working with the subject and using the methods. It means taking a step back to see the larger picture of what goes on in learning, and how the relationship between students and teachers influences learning. It also means attending to small details which can in turn change the bigger picture. Teacher development is a continuous process of transforming human potential into human performance, a process that is never finished.

The Teacher Development Series offers perspectives on learning that embrace topic, method and person as parts of one larger interacting whole. We aim to help you, the teacher, trainer or academic manager to stretch your awareness not only of what you do and how you do it, but also of how you affect your learners and colleagues. This will enable you to extract more from your own experience, both as it happens and in retrospect, and to become more actively involved in your own continuous learning. The books themselves will focus on new treatments of familiar subects as well as areas that are just emerging as subjects of the future.

The series represents work that is in progress rather than finished or closed. The authors are themselves exploring, and invite you to bring your own experience to the study of these books while at the same time learning from the experiences of others. We encourage you to observe, value and understand your own experience, and to evaluate and integrate relevant external practice and knowledge into your own internal evolving model of effective teaching and learning.

Adrian Underhill

About the authors

Graham Impey

I am the managing director of International Language Centres (UK) Ltd.

ILC UK comprises:

International House Hastings
A year-round school which offers a range of General English, Examination, Executive and Teacher Training Courses.

ILC Vacation Courses
More than 30 junior and adult centres in the UK, Ireland and the USA.

I am also a director and minority shareholder of ILC Group Ltd which has schools and contracts in the Czech Republic, France, the Gulf and the UK.

I started teaching English as a foreign language in 1979 and have held a number of director of studies and managerial posts before taking up my current position in 1988.

Nic Underhill

I have taught English and managed ELT programmes in Britain, France and Kuwait. After teaching at International House, Hastings and other schools in the south of England, I directed the ILC English Language Training Programme at Kuwait Oil Company. I worked for two years as director of ILC Paris, then moved back to Britain to become the first education officer of ARELS. I am currently the head of the TESOL Centre at Sheffield Business School, part of Sheffield Hallam University.

I have written two other books: *Testing Spoken Language* (Cambridge University Press 1987) which won the English Speaking Union Prize for Methodology in 1988, and *Focus on Studying in Britain* (Macmillan 1991). I have edited the IATEFL ELT Management Newsletter since its inception in 1989.

I am convinced that good management is essentially an attitude of mind allied to practical experience, rather than a set of formal skills. A greater awareness of management issues enables all staff to do their jobs more effectively and to contribute to the forward development of their institution.

Introduction to *The ELT Manager's Handbook*

THIS BOOK is about managing and running English language teaching (ELT) programmes.

We, the authors, are not management theorists. We are practitioners, with many years' experience of managing English language programmes, and it is this practical on-the-ground experience that we hope will come through. The topic areas in this book are therefore management activities to think about and act on rather than academic disciplines to learn about.

Who are you? Who is the book written for?

- people whose job includes day-to-day management of an English language teaching programme, especially in smaller schools where the management is not highly formalized and specialized;
- people who are well-established in supervisory roles, but have felt the need to look above the routine of daily administration to consider the longer-term issues of management;
- people who are new, or relatively new to, or preparing for, a management role;
- people who want to understand more and know more, but may not actually exercise a management role.

We want to write for anyone who wants a better insight, to become better informed, to know more, to be able to talk about or contribute to the management of their institution. We believe that the more staff know and contribute to the daily discussion about how things should be done, the more stimulating the institution will be as a place to work in.

What are the fundamental principles on which the book is based?

1 **The 'people-centred approach'.** People are the key to successful management: the provision of high-quality ELT is a meeting of people and minds. Even among traditionally labour-intensive service industries, teaching is unusually intangible and dependent on the motivation and good will of all staff; successful interaction is all, and it is often an interaction between people of different cultural backgrounds.

2 **Successful management requires a clear sense of direction**. If you don't know where you're supposed to be going, how can you get there? This applies both to your personal development as an actual or potential manager, and to the management of the institute you work in. Defining your goals may seem to be an exercise in stating the obvious, but usually it's anything but obvious when you actually try to do it. It is a process of discovery that facilitates management in general, and decision-making in particular, all the way down the line.

3 **Successful management is unseen**. From the customer's point of view, there should be a seamless continuity from first contact through to course delivery to farewell and follow-up. The customer interacts with the reception staff; the teachers, obviously; the director of studies or operations manager, perhaps; but

the senior management may only become visible, other than in a courtesy role, when things go wrong. As well as the obvious perspective, you need to look at the whole service through the client's eyes, to see where the seams are likely to appear.

4 Although there are many different aspects to management – personnel, finance, promotion, etc – these are different facets of the overall whole and not fundamental divisions. **Successful management is not only indivisible, it positively looks for the interconnections**, between education and finance, for example, or between personnel and marketing, and it looks for ways to exploit them. One of the roles of managers may even be to make themselves redundant as 'professional managers' by promoting a culture in which management becomes the right and responsibility of everybody.

5 **Successful management is not an academic discipline**. We can stand back, theorize and speculate, but ultimately management takes place in real time in the real world. Hence our emphasis throughout on the application of our experience and of your experience, through real-life situations and examples.

What assumptions have been made?

We have assumed that you, the reader, have a sound TEFL background, so that no explanation of pedagogic issues is necessary.

We have assumed that if not directly involved in school or programme management, you have at least some access to management information about the institution where you work, in order to be able to apply some of the ideas.

Obviously, not every idea will work in every school. We assume that you will know enough about how your institution works, or can find out enough, to be able to make a reasoned judgement as to whether particular ideas are appropriate or not.

We have assumed *either* that you work in an atmosphere where making suggestions is welcome, and where asking about and questioning the established way of doing things is not regarded with suspicion; *or* that you'd like your school to move more towards such openness. We hope this book can help in that process.

Chapter 1 Why does your school exist?

Introduction

Management in general, and decision-making in particular, is easier if you know where you're going: if you have a set of objectives defining the goals you are supposed to be working towards. It is much more straightforward to plan a sales campaign or to update your school's recruitment policy if you have at the back of your mind what the long-term goals are, and can take action or make decisions in the short term consistent with those long-term goals.

For example, you might be faced with a decision about the allocation of priorities between different projects – a new self-access centre or the development of a secretarial skills course, or how much money to invest in re-training staff to teach young children. Reference to your institution's long-term aims will not affect the short-term needs, but it will tell you which projects are more closely consistent with the general direction and which are not.

Your colleagues will work together better if they know and understand the long-term aims. People have a need to know why they are there. On a practical level, they will be able to work more efficiently and more autonomously, with less need for constant internal cross-reference: 'There's a woman on the phone talking about teacher-training for children. Is that something we're interested in?' could and should be: 'A woman rang to tell us about teacher-training for children, so I asked her to send us more information.'

Externally, it is much easier to present a concise and memorable description of your institution for any kind of promotional purpose if you have an explicit statement of aims to work from; literally 'memorable', because other people will remember a simple clear explanation that includes a sense of direction.

If your school already has clearly-defined, agreed and understood objectives, congratulations! – you're in a small minority. It may still be useful for you to look at the following section (especially if you did not contribute to the formulation of the objectives, or possibly may not even personally agree with them) to see how closely they are actually being realized in practice, rather than displayed in bright lights and then largely ignored. In contrast, most of us work in institutions where the aims have not been clearly specified, and this makes our jobs harder.

The purpose of this short chapter is to set you thinking about the kind of place you work in (Section 1), and so to help in the formulation or evaluation of a statement of aims (Section 2). Working through these activities will clarify what you want from this book. We can't promise to provide all the answers, but you are more likely to find what you're looking for if you have taken five minutes to focus consciously on the reality of your current work situation and have a clear view of how you personally want to develop and move forward.

The first section contains a series of tasks to help crystallize your thoughts about your workplace. Following each task, there are some comments: each school and institution is different, so there can be no right answers, but there are clearly going to be individual and collective values and practices that are more or less desirable in a particular workplace.

If it is appropriate, you can use these tasks as a focusing exercise for a group of your colleagues to work through together. If you can arrange to meet outside the normal work schedule, preferably off the school premises and in an informal atmosphere, it will be worth taking the extra time and effort to elicit everybody's opinions fully in neutral and relaxed surroundings. Four to six people is a comfortable size, and you may want to set a time limit on each task, first working individually, then comparing notes. You may find that an enormous amount of discussion is generated, and perhaps a wide range of conflicting opinions. This suggests that however amicable the working atmosphere may be, people are pulling in different directions, rather than working toward a common goal, and that a great deal of further discussion may be needed to create a sense of focus.

1 What kind of place do you work in?

Look at these tasks and think out or write down short answers.

Task 1

First of all, what is the **profile** of your school or institution? Try to summarize it in a single sentence for the benefit of someone who knows nothing about it. Where is it? Who does it serve? Who owns it? Is it in the private or state sector? Is English language teaching the main or only activity, or is it a sideline in a larger organization or institution?

Commentary ■ ■ ■

The profile of the school or institution is obviously of fundamental importance in defining how it is managed. For example, how is the management of change regarded? Is it the stuff of everyday life for colleagues to participate in, or is it something to discuss at the next management committee meeting, with the decisions taken subsequently disseminated? Because there are so many different types of ELT institution, there cannot be any correct answers to these questions, nor to most of the others posed in this book, but it is still vital that you ask the questions (aloud, if you can!).

Here are some examples of different profiles to illustrate the enormous diversity of English language teaching programmes:

1　A private language school located in a native English-speaking country, catering almost exclusively to students who come from 'abroad', owned and managed as a single institution by the resident principal/director.
2　A private language school located in a non-native English-speaking country, catering largely to local students wishing to improve their English, but also to local and perhaps incoming students learning the local language (or perhaps a range of non-native languages).

3 An educational institution in the state or private sector, where English language teaching is a major activity, but not the primary activity, which is to prepare students of partly or entirely non-native English-speaking backgrounds through the medium of English for other academic or vocational qualifications (for example, a teacher-training college or sixth-form college).

4 A governmental department or inter-governmental organization providing language training for its staff, either for use 'on-site' or in preparation for posting to other countries (for example, a training school for diplomats, or foreign office or defence department staff).

5 A large private entity, such as an industrial or commercial organization, whose primary activity is not educational. For example, a bank or an oil company whose employees need English in different skills to differing degrees in order to carry out their duties.

6 A state sector college where English language teaching is one among many academic activities; or may be only for pre-sessional or in-sessional support, to enable students of other disciplines to make the most of their studies.

7 A private language school as in 1 or 2 above but run entirely by its staff on a co-operative basis.

8 A charitable organization training volunteers to operate in remote areas, or local staff to act as interpreters or as a basis for further training in health, agricultural or technological fields.

In this great diversity, each institution has its own unique profile and its own management challenges and rewards. This profile is reflected in the varying degrees to which the different topic areas of this book will be relevant. A school catering entirely for local students will have no need for an accommodation service; a subsidiary of a larger organization or chain of schools may have little local responsibility for formulating strategy or setting prices; a training centre in an industrial or commercial enterprise might have no external sales activity.

However, in many cases, these functions will still be carried out by someone in the organization, in some form, somewhere, and if the immediate staff of the local programme have no contribution to make or are not consulted at all, then perhaps they should be. As a matter of personal development, they can certainly consider the issues involved and how they might apply to the immediate situation. Even where they are not directly applicable, we hope other sections will at least be interesting to read and think about.

As well as areas of difference, there must be substantial areas of overlap too: 'common core' ELT management, if you like, that is practised everywhere, albeit under local conditions, but with recognizably the same basic skills. Among these are:

- operations management, the day-to-day organization of teaching programmes;
- leadership, motivation and support of all staff;
- strategy formulation and execution;
- financial management: essentially, getting value for money;
- programme evaluation and staff appraisal. ■

Task 2

What is the management structure in your school? Sketch out a simple diagram showing job titles, who reports to whom and who supervises whom. Draw in arrows to show how much daily communication there is between people: use thickness to illustrate the volume of everyday contact.

Is the structure hierarchical and 'top-down', with decisions being handed down the chain of command and reports being handed back up? Are there several levels in the hierarchy, or is it a flattened pyramid, with relatively few levels, but with a lot of people reporting to one manager or principal?

To what extent is there a sense of collegiality, of everybody working together with a common sense of purpose, irrespective of their title or position? Is there a clear communication gap between teaching and administrative staff? Does it make any sense to talk of the 'front-line' people, who are directly responsible for delivering the services you sell, and who are backed up by other staff, such as the management, in the back room?

Commentary ■ ■ ■

Is management a set of skills or is it a state of mind? The conventional, hierarchical view of management is that it is something that is done by some people (managers) to other people (staff); in a school, the manager might typically be called director or principal, with some management duties assigned to a director of studies or delegated to others.

This traditional view sees management as a full-time job in its own right, which is necessarily higher in the hierarchy than the staff 'at the chalkface' whose working lives are controlled by the management's decisions. Enlightened managers may consult their staff about the decisions, but ultimately it is the managers who make and implement those decisions. However enlightened they may be, 'management' is an activity that only they engage in, while others are controlled by it.

One alternative to this traditional, hierarchical model is to take the top-down hierarchy and turn it through 90 degrees, so that instead of being at the bottom of the diagram, the 'front-line' people are at the sharp end, at the 'interface' with the customers, and other staff are behind them:

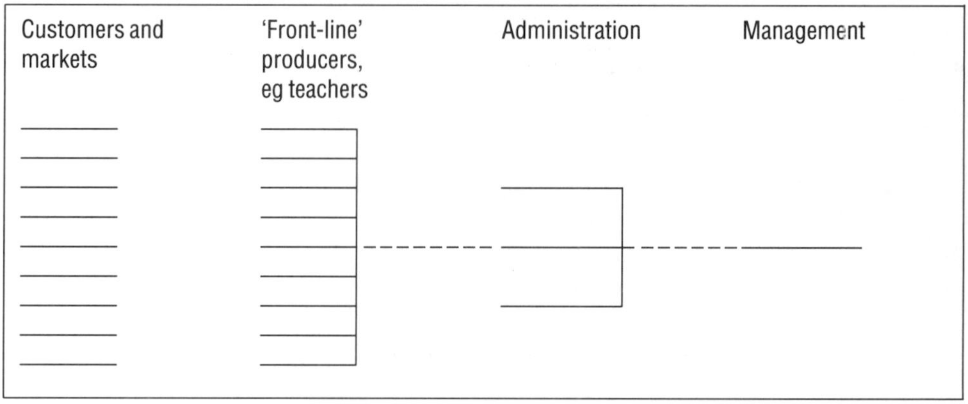

Fig 1.1: The 'front line' (after Charles 1993)

Who are the 'front-line' people in your school? Teachers, mainly, but anyone who is directly involved in delivering the services you sell and dealing with clients. Teachers, all the time; reception and other staff, part of the time; managers, scarcely at all! This produces some interesting points of view:

- It emphasizes that the 'front-line' people are really crucial in an organization, not only the managers (managers get paid more).
- It removes the hierarchy of superiority that places a manager 'above' a 'front-line' person.
- It emphasizes that although we may have different jobs we are all working to a common purpose.

So what do the 'front-line' people have to do with management? With a shared sense of purpose, and a clear sense of their own role in achieving that purpose, they *are* the management. It may not be only to the benefit of the individual teacher's professional development to ask more, know more and contribute more to the direction and management of the institution, it will ultimately be to the benefit of the organization as a whole. ■

Task 3 Are you and your colleagues 'switched on' or 'switched off'?

Which of the following profiles better characterizes your organization?

1 *Are the objectives decided*
   a by interaction with those who have to carry them out?
   b unilaterally, at board or management level?

2 *In communication with senior staff,*
   a are truthfulness and openness genuinely welcomed?
   b do you have to be careful what you say to whom?

3 *At the end of the day, are staff judged by*
   a the achievement of results consistent with the objectives set?
   b the form of company behaviour (following rules, processing paperwork, etc)?

4 *When an unpleasant or difficult decision has to be taken,*
   a is it thrashed out, at whatever cost in time and temper?
   b is it sometimes just left hanging, in the hope that 'something will turn up'?

5 *To introduce an innovation or experiment with variation of routine procedure,*
   a is there sufficient 'headroom' for an individual to try it out?
   b does the decision have to be passed upward to someone to take authority?

6 *Does the remuneration system reward*
   a the people who keep things going?
   b the golden boys or girls of the moment?

7 *Are the demands made on people*
   a sufficient to stretch them?
   b at times quite unrealistic?

(after Harvey-Jones 1988 pp 65–80)

Commentary ■ ■ ■

This is based on a distinction made by John Harvey-Jones between companies that 'switch on' their staff, and those that 'switch them off'. The **a** options, generally, switch people on: they enable staff to operate without fear or favour, to participate in the formulation of objectives and to seek the best ways to achieve them; in the process, they also gain confidence and effectiveness and enjoy high morale. The **b** options switch people off: they reward the dutiful employee who follows company procedures, plays safe rather than innovates, takes his or her cue by looking inwards rather than outwards, and at the end of the day does not feel responsible for the achievement of the objectives. ■

Task 4 The role of the teacher

How is the role of the teachers seen in your institution? (By teachers themselves and by others.)

1 *Is the perspective of the teacher*
 a limited to the immediate in time and place?

 b embracing the broader social context of education?

2 *Are classroom events perceived*
 a in isolation?

 b in relation to the school's policies and goals?

3 *Are teachers*
 a introspective with regard to methods?

 b comparing methods with those of colleagues and with reports of practice?

4 *Is value placed*
 a on autonomy in the classroom?

 b on professional collaboration?

5 *Is there*
 a limited involvement in non-teaching professional activities?

 b high involvement in non-teaching professional activities?

6 *Do teachers read professional literature*
 a infrequently?

 b regularly?

7 *Is involvement in in-service work*
 a limited and confined to practical courses?

 b extensive and including courses of a theoretical nature?

8 *Is teaching seen*
 a as an intuitive activity?

 b as a rational activity?

(after Hoyle 1975 p 318)

Commentary ■ ■ ■

These questions are based on a distinction between *restricted professionality* and *extended professionality*. In each case, answer **a** is characteristic of restricted professionality, while answer **b** represents extended professionality. The distinction is artificial and simplistic, but the underlying point is central to this book. It is that there is one sense of professionalism for teachers which is restricted to what happens in the classroom, where teachers have traditionally enjoyed a higher degree of independence in determining the style, and often the content, of their teaching. A wider sense of professionalism, however, would extend outside the classroom to include a greater say in the decision-making and management of the institution; as in Task 2 above, each individual would become a manager in his or her own right. To enable teaching staff to make this transition from the role typified by the **a** answers to that of the **b** answers, they will need much greater knowledge of how things work and many more opportunities to acquire and practise the necessary management skills. One purpose of this book is to enable teachers to play a more significant role in the management of the institutions where they work. ■

Task 5 Change

Think of three or four recent examples of changes that have been made – one or two major changes and one or two more minor ones. How were the decisions made in each case?

Generally, who decides what directions the school will move in? Who can participate in such decisions? How easy is it in practice for a member of staff to propose and promote an idea for genuine discussion? What is the procedure for deciding on and implementing changes, for example in the courses being offered? Is it:

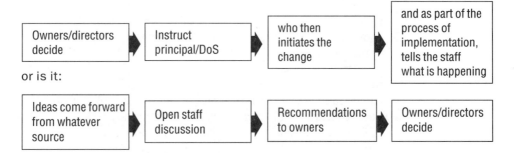

or is it:

or is it a combination of these, or something else?

Commentary ■ ■ ■

Attitudes to change are vital to any discussion of management. The circumstances in which we live and work are constantly changing. We are continuously adapting to these changing circumstances in order to make the most of them; we try to anticipate future changes so that we can accommodate ourselves to them.

On a professional level too, we have to change in order to survive. For all language programmes, there is the constant threat that our competitors will get an edge over us, will find out how to exploit that lead successfully, and will take business away from us. It is no exaggeration to say that a large part of management is about managing change and maintaining the impetus for continuous evolution.

Examples of changing global circumstances in our field might be:

- the development of new markets as people in 'new' countries acquire the freedom and resources to travel abroad, and the desire to learn English;
- the evolution of more integrated trading blocks such as the European Community and ultimately the 'world market', with English as the principal means of business communication;
- cycles of relative prosperity in different countries and the status of the English language in each country.

At the other extreme, examples of changing local circumstances might be:

- an increased demand for one course and a drop in bookings for another;
- a sudden drop in income, requiring an urgent re-evaluation of budgets and future plans;
- changes in ministry requirements, education legislation (eg teaching of English in primary schools) or recognition criteria;
- fiscal changes (eg tax incentives for language training for company personnel).

Change, then, is not something that happens from time to time, an inconvenience that we have to put up with; it is an integral and central part of the manager's concern. As the person in the driving seat, we may be able to see things coming which our passengers cannot. The art of managing change is to keep everybody together, working in the same direction, while still responding fast enough to the changing circumstances around us.

Here are some suggestions for managing change:

1 Identify who is likely to be affected by a particular change.
2 Find out and take into account the different points of view of everybody concerned.
3 Involve everybody concerned in the discussion. You may not expect unanimity, or perhaps even seek it, but always ask for opinions.
4 Encourage people to express their worries and objections. If opposition cannot be aired, it remains a potential threat to the success of the change.
5 Talk to individuals privately about their particular concerns. See if these are hiding other, underlying issues which have not been expressed in public.
6 Within reason, spend as much time as you can at the discussion stage. Allow a group consensus to develop to push things forward. The more agreement you can achieve in advance, the greater commitment there will be to implement the change, and the faster it will happen. ∎

Task 6 Who gains what from the school's activities?

Draw in lines, real or imaginary, from the people in the left-hand column to the benefits on the right. Use thickness to indicate, in your own opinion, the size of the benefit:

Who ...	... gains what?
owner(s)	learning English
principal/director	professional/personal development
staff	cultural awareness
students	money
local community	job satisfaction
parent institution (eg college or	servicing other departments/ needs
corporation)	other benefits: _____
parent institution staff	
other people: _____	

Is this a satisfactory distribution of benefits? If you could wave a magic wand, what additional benefits would you like to accrue to which people?

Commentary ■ ■ ■

The aim of this task is to identify what you yourself see as the most urgent problems of human resources. It does not mean that you will necessarily be able to do anything about them immediately. However, if you have any say in the running of the organization, then knowing how you would like to spread the benefits will help you to work towards that reallocation, and to recognize opportunities to persuade others to work in the same direction. ■

2 Formulating a statement of aims

Now that you have worked through the tasks above, you should be in a better position to formulate an explicit set of aims for your institution, to answer the question 'Why are you there?' Whether you will have the authority or encouragement to do so is a different matter! Owners/directors may not consider it a necessary or worthwhile task and if you are not able to enlist their support, then clearly the exercise has less face validity. However, it can still be useful as a staff development exercise, and if it produces positive results, you can subsequently put them forward for consideration and, hopefully, adoption by the owners/directors.

The phrase 'statement of aims' is being used here in a generic sense. It is fashionable now to use the rather pompous term 'mission statement' to describe a broad outline of a company's philosophy in terms of its business, the business environment and its internal organization. A statement of aims in the sense used here might indeed include such an outline, but it would also be more specific in setting objectives, and therefore more immediately useful. Where a mission statement is essentially an abstract of why an organization exists, a statement of aims should be a more practical summary of where it is supposed to be going. It is just as likely to fail to meet its aims as it is to fail to live up to its mission, but at least it should be easier to determine whether or not it has failed!

The statement of aims should provide the focal point to generate a sense of common purpose and direction that allows diverse groups of people to work towards a common cause. It is particularly important, where there is a large proportion of professional staff with considerable freedom in determining how to achieve the aims of the organization, to make those aims explicit and agreed, even if it seems like an exercise in stating the obvious. Often, it isn't obvious at all.

The statement of aims must therefore be a clear and concise statement about the purpose and goals of the school or institution. It should be a source of information for staff and other people, and it should provide a valuable reference point against which to check strategic proposals in areas such as marketing and employment policy. It should remain reasonably stable over time: obviously, schools need to change direction like any other business in response to changing circumstances, but you should not need to redefine your general aims every year.

Core components

Two obvious components are, firstly, that private companies will want to make explicit their *financial aim*: otherwise, they are understating their commitment to their own long-term survival, and shareholders or other investors are not going to be impressed. Secondly, organizations operating in a particular field will want to specify that field as their *zone of activity*.

The financial aim for a private company may be in the form of an explicit growth target or market share. To state that its goal is 'to maximize the return on investment' is only being honest; this is probably the real primary objective of most language schools, but our inherited attitude to education as something that shouldn't be tainted with blatantly commercial activity prevents us from saying so too loudly. Wouldn't it be better to get it out in the open?

Where an educational programme is part of a state-sector institution or a charitable trust, its financial aim will normally be to cover its full costs and allow investment for the future.

Optional components

Beyond the core components, there is a wide variety of other possible elements, and this is where you can show, for both internal and external audiences, what your real philosophy or raison d'être is. Staff welfare including remuneration, motivation and a commitment to their development, and different aspects of social responsibility, eg environmental issues, are common here.

Other possible elements are value for money; standards of service; equality of access and opportunity for staff and students; commitment to and investment in research; contribution to the local community; and co-operation with other institutions or agencies.

Tips for producing a statement of aims

IT DOESN'T MATTER what you call it – *mission, aims, objectives, purpose, philosophy* – the important point is to focus people's conscious attention on why the organization exists and where it is going.

THE PURPOSE OF AN ORGANIZATION is usually defined by its owners, and they obviously have a major say in its formulation. However:

… everybody who works there should have an opportunity to contribute to the formulation of a statement of aims.

A SERIES OF MEETINGS over a period of time will be needed to reap the benefits of this consultation.

START WITH A STAFF BRAINSTORMING SESSION, to generate a list of all the possible components that people think could be included. At this stage, any ideas should be allowed.

HAVE A BALLOT to vote on the possible components, to find out what the staff see as the most important objectives.

TAKE THE OPPORTUNITY also to ask customers whose opinions you value, such as students past or present or company clients, what they would expect to see as the institution's goals.

DEVELOP A DRAFT – a job for just one or two people! – try it out, revise it, edit it, and above all, try to shorten it without losing anything important. The fewer words, the more impact.

ABOVE ALL, BE CLEAR WHY YOU ARE DOING IT. An organization that has a clear sense of direction and purpose is more likely to survive and succeed than one that doesn't.

Commentary ■ ■ ■

- Where typically the purpose has never even been discussed, a lot of time and effort may be wasted by this lack of focus, with people pulling in different directions.
- The aims may be thought to be commonly understood, and so not need to be made explicit. However, making explicit what everybody thinks they know implicitly can be a useful exercise, and often you find that the unspoken assumptions do not in fact entirely overlap – far from it!
- The most useful part of creating a statement of aims may be the exercise itself as a team-building activity. The exact formula of words that is produced may ultimately be unimportant, if the process of producing it in itself engenders a genuine debate which in turn creates the focus that is lacking. However, if you are unable to reach agreement at all, it suggests you have some serious problems ahead!
- The owners or managers may be surprised to find that in open discussion about the goals of an organization, staff may have novel and different ideas that if adopted can stimulate the forward development of the company and its staff.
- If an institution is a state college, a charitable trust or a non-profit-making organization, there are no owners, in the usual sense, to make policy; but there is just as great a need, perhaps even greater if the immediate programme is part of a much larger institution, for a clear focus to give a sense of direction. ■

Chapter 2 Marketing and promotion

Introduction

Marketing means finding out what people want, then producing it and offering it to them. It is both a *specific activity* which needs to be carried out as a vital stage in the development of a new product, and a *continuous process* that is an integral part of everyday management activity.

In a manufacturing company, the marketing department pinpoints a new product that could be successfully developed and introduced. The research and development department designs it; then the production department makes it, the publicity department promotes it, and the sales department sells it.

In reality, you are probably all of these departments, and several others too. This is good, because you can bypass all the problems of communication between the different departments. At the same time, it may be helpful to think consciously which hat you are wearing at any one moment, so as not to confuse marketing with other related activities.

What marketing *is*:

- being customer-oriented, taking the market as the starting point;
- integrating a number of different functions, such as planning which courses or other services to market; designing and packaging them; deciding on the price structure; promoting and presenting them in various ways; following up;
- developing a strategy that concentrates effort on meeting the stated aims of the organization, so that effort is focused and not wasted (after Cameron et. al. 1988 p 12).

Marketing views the entire business process as 'consisting of a tightly integrated effort to discover, create, arouse, and satisfy customer needs' (Levitt, in Cameron et. al. 1988 p 12).

What marketing *is not*:

- getting your name known (this is publicity);
- preparing specific courses on demand (course design);
- getting people to buy your courses (sales) or represent you (agency);
- going to nice places in the hope of making useful contacts (junketing).

1   What is 'the market'?

The market is what people want and are willing to buy. This is not necessarily the same as:

a what people are trying to sell – because the producers have misread the market, or for whatever reason are unable to adapt their product to the market. For example, a school that insists on rigid 'terms' of ten to twelve weeks, when customers are wanting shorter courses (or vice-versa!);

b what people are already buying – because they cannot find what they really want, and are buying as a second choice. For example, they may only have been exposed to local publicity for courses taught in monolingual groups, but when offered the option, appreciate readily that multilingual classes may be preferable;

c what customers think they want – because they may not have realized the range of products and services available, or appreciated the finer points that distinguish them. For example, the benefit of a really good teacher compared with an ordinary one, or the benefit of learning in a small group rather than the large classes they have previously experienced.

We are using the word market here as a metaphor; it is a convenient short-hand, conjuring up an image of buyers going to a certain place to meet sellers, looking around the wares to find what they want, making an informed decision and then negotiating a purchase. Like all metaphors, it is over-simplistic. In this case, it ignores the facts that:

- some buyers never meet a representative of the course provider before they decide to purchase; they may be a long way away, and if they meet anyone it might be a local teacher or an agent (the local 'retailer');
- even if they visit the school personally before they buy, it is very unlikely that they will actually have the opportunity to sample the product, eg to sit in on or participate in a class;
- they may in fact get very little accurate information to work on, and may well be unaware of the huge range of schools and courses available;
- they may make a decision on unpredictable criteria (location, image, personal convenience of dates and times, etc).

The market for EFL courses is characterized by:

> **widespread distribution:** geographical; by age: primary, secondary, tertiary, adult; by sector (state vs private); by purpose; etc

but this...

> **enormous worldwide demand** is almost entirely met by small or medium-sized schools, state schools and colleges; there are few large players.

So classically in a free market, there is...

> **strong competition**

and therefore...

> **generally low profits**

Given the nature of the business, there is...

> **a low start-up cost:** virtually no investment is required in fixed plant or raw materials, and premises can be rented as needed

and

> **low client awareness:** the difficulty for the non-expert, and non-speaker, of distinguishing between nearly identical claims from many different schools

but there is also...

> **poor marketing intelligence**
> (but see Sections 2 and 3 below)

and

> **conflicting goals:** different students want English for different purposes; even for one student, why she thinks she wants to attend a course, why her parents/sponsors pay for her to learn, and why she actually ends up using English may be entirely different

and in native-speaker countries, a need to offer to a competitive standard:

> **a complex packages of services** such as accommodation activities, excursions, sports, airport transfers, etc as well as tuition

TIP **'Study the side roads even when walking straight.'** Market research may throw up opportunities that are not directly to do with English language teaching – publishing, selling books, arranging travel or accommodation, selling train or theatre tickets, selling on commission courses in other subjects or at other schools, etc (see Chapter 6, Section 3: 'How do you increase non-teaching revenue?'). Such activities are outside the regular scope of a language school or programme, but may be interesting for you to consider, particularly if they complement your language courses – they offer students something extra and/or generate extra revenue. At the least, they may enable you to offer an unusual range or combination of services, so acting as a stimulus to sales of your main courses.

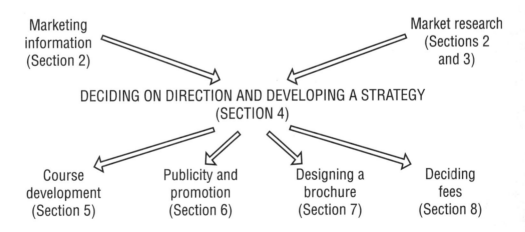

Fig. 2.1: Planning a marketing campaign (numbers in brackets refer to sections in this chapter)

2 What marketing information is available?

There is almost no publicly available information on the market for English language tuition. Since the ELT market is so widespread, and the provision so fragmented with so many small schools jealously protecting their own contacts and sources of students, there is little pooling of information.

Having said this, there are some sources of more or less useful information, which depend very largely on where you are and what local, regional or national systems there are for collating and disseminating details on the demand for and supply of language teaching.

For schools in native-speaker countries, much of the useful information is tourism-based rather than specifically ELT-related:

- Reports from national tourist authorities, for example the British Tourist Authority, who produce detailed reports for marketing purposes on particular regions and countries. National and regional tourist authorities also produce periodic statistics for visitors by country and type of visit (eg length of stay).
- Reports and initiatives by other government bodies, such as the English Language Promotion Unit of the British Council, sometimes country-specific, sometimes more general, eg 'Talking to Agents.'
- Reports produced by private companies, eg 'Students Talking', based on focus group research among students at schools in Britain.
- Information and statistics produced by trade associations, such as ARELS and BASCELT in Britain or ELICOS in Australia. This information may be restricted to members only, eg the Marketing Information Network operated by EFL Services in the UK. If you cannot join such an information service, consider starting your own locally.
- The ELT trade press (eg the *EFL Gazette* and *Language Travel Gazette*); also the travel trade press, which although often of marginal relevance, may signal major changes in the opening up or decline of particular geographic markets.
- The general business press. This is worth watching for language and language travel-related articles, and magazines such as *The Economist* also produce detailed reports on particular markets; however, these tend to be expensive and offer little more than you can find out for yourself.

What market research is practicable and useful?

Because of the lack of reliable, up-to-date, published information, most marketing information is gathered 'by hand' by individual contacts with people on the ground. Few schools are large enough to set up a professional market research programme, but there is a lot of research that can easily be done at an informal level:

1 Talk to your students.
2 Talk to agents, both yours and others.
3 Talk to tourist authorities, representatives of organizations like the British Council, trade or commercial attachés at embassies.
4 Talk to teachers at conferences and exhibitions.
5 Talk to your competitors: what impression do they, their staff and students, have of your school?

6 Collect and analyze your student statistics – see Section 3, pp 18–22).

As you see, all this involves a lot of talking! Writing to people, for example with a questionnaire asking for their views, may not produce much of a response unless you have some kind of incentive, such as a discount; but it's often worth trying (once, at least).

Here's a look at each of these ideas in more detail.

Students

Students are a convenient audience, and you can structure the information-gathering exercise to make it a useful (and extra free) communication exercise for them. By definition, your students are already customers; they are the ones that were able to come, or for whom the course was right. Bear in mind that you want to know even more why the ones that got away didn't come, or found your competitors' courses and services more attractive.

Two ways to capitalize on market research among your existing students are **student questionnaires** and **student committees**. In both cases, they may have another main purpose, but you can still exploit their information-gathering potential.

Student questionnaires

The purpose of student questionnaires depends on when in the course they are administered:

On arrival: It is important to try to establish what students' first impressions are of your school. First impressions last! Although it seems a bit unnecessary to give an immediate questionnaire, some questions about first impressions could perhaps be combined with an existing questionnaire about needs analysis or language-learning background; or could be integrated into an informal oral test.

Mid-course: Offers an opportunity for airing problems after an initial settling in period, but while there is still time to do something about them. Ideally, a week to two weeks after the start of the course, depending on intensity. But if you raise expectations by asking questions, you must be ready to follow up any problems raised.

End-of-course: It may now be too late to change anything, but it is useful to get final feedback. What kind of impression are the students leaving with? What do they want to get off their chest? If there are grievances that they don't air until the last day when it's too late to remedy them, why didn't they bring them up earlier?

After-course: Arguably, the most accurate and durable reactions are those elicited some time after the course has finished. When the students are back in their normal working or studying lives, how do they view the course? There is a promotional benefit, too: experience shows that generally students' reactions are more favourable after a period of time, presumably because they have had time for the petty annoyances and culture conflicts to be seen in proportion, and to be viewed against the positive features of the experience as a whole. Combine this with a follow-up offer, eg a re-enrolment discount, or a regular newsletter, or a copy of your new brochure and prices.

In terms of the format of the questionnaire, as well as the obvious 'tick boxes' or 'award points on a scale from 1 to 5', there are more open-ended types of question that elicit generally positive reactions and provide useful marketing information:

- Ask why they chose your school.
- Ask what advice they would give to other students coming there.
- Encourage the keeping of 'learner diaries' which record the learner's reactions to all aspects of their stay, not just the lessons; and arrange for this feedback to be regularly 'sampled', eg by the class teacher.
- Find out which features of your local town or region the students found most interesting (don't forget to put 'shopping' on the list of favourite pastimes). Then exploit this information for your future promotional material: 'Our students really enjoy the convenience of a major shopping centre on the doorstep ...'

Student committees

If you have a student committee, you can use it to get marketing information. If you don't have a committee, set one up, with one or two representatives from each class, and staff from the welfare and social departments as well as teaching and management. It should meet quite informally perhaps once or twice a month to discuss recent and planned developments in the school, and any matters that the staff or students wish to bring up. It is good:

- as a source of consumer response – how do students see your school and all its services? Do they respond as you think or hope they do? Dare you find out?
- as a testbed for new ideas – ask the consumers before you innovate;
- as a 'neutral ground' on which to explore the current mood/feeling/atmosphere;
- for acting as an informal 'early warning' channel of communication which allows students to make comments and you to act on them without the awkwardness and embarrassment of a real complaint;
- for encouraging communication between staff in different departments;
- as a real and authentic communication exercise for students!

Agents

Research is one of the three main reasons for regular visits to agents (along with encouraging them to send more students this year *and* to pay for the ones they sent last year!). Rather than trying to pack everything into an hour, then on to the next appointment, it is worth allowing enough time to have a good chat, perhaps over a meal or a drink. A successful day is measured by the amount you have learned, not the number of people you have visited. Talking on the phone is a quick and relatively cheap way of keeping in touch, but it is difficult to have a frank and open-ended conversation on the phone unless it is someone you already know well.

While this information will always be anecdotal, you tend to find that by talking to as many people as possible, general patterns of opinion emerge about how a particular region/country or a particular market is looking (eg the Taiwanese market for long-stay courses is getting stronger, or companies seem to be cutting back on non-essential language training). There will always be someone who flatly and authoritatively contradicts what others say – your job is to decide whether that person is more perceptive than everybody else, or just plain wrong!

Tourist authorities and government organizations

Tourist authorities and representatives of organizations like the British Council, trade or commercial attachés at embassies, Chambers of Commerce, bilateral trade associations, etc may be in a position to have either a good view of general market trends in a particular country or detailed statistical information about language travel, or both. How useful they are depends on how their jobs are structured and how much time and resources they have available for gathering intelligence. How you approach them is also important: you can 'cultivate' someone, in a positive sense, by giving them feedback on any contacts they pass to you, so that you are giving as well as taking, and the exchange of marketing information becomes a two-way process.

Teachers

In some countries, school teachers, whom you can talk to at conferences and exhibitions, are the front-line agents that recruit a lot of language travel students from among their own students or locally in their town or area. In all countries they have very good first-hand knowledge of the local provision of ELT, although this may be limited to the particular sector they are working in. From a long-term view, however, the strengths and weaknesses of the system they are implementing now will be reflected in the strengths and weaknesses of your potential students in five or ten years' time. Wouldn't it be useful to know about them now?

The competition

You can get a lot of useful information from other schools in the same town or area, either on an informal basis or from regular meetings to discuss issues of common interest. For many people, the real benefit of attending meetings and conferences of national associations is not so much the formal business that is conducted, but rather comes from the trade gossip. Choose somebody you trust, invite them to come and spend a couple of hours looking over your school, and offer to do the same for them. Then swap your impressions of what you have seen.

One obvious further source of marketing information is your own institution, and in particular a statistical analysis of your business. So ...

3   What kind of records should you keep?
What can you do with them?

The short answer is that you should collect information that you have identified a genuine need for, where the cost of collection does not outweigh the benefit, and where you will actually use this information to help decide your future strategy and marketing plan.

We are talking here about student statistics expressed in some kind of 'student-unit' (see below), not financial statistics expressed purely in terms of money, although you may want to convert the student-units to income at some point, for example for forward-planning and budgeting purposes.

It is of crucial importance to define for yourself *why* you want to collect statistics, and *what information* you want to get from them.

Good reasons for collecting statistics:

- They allow you to compare performance of different courses and sources historically over time and with other schools, to help you evaluate the success of a course or school.
- They provide vital objective information for making strategic management decisions, for example by detecting trends early on.
- There may be legislative, fiscal or regulatory requirements to submit detailed information about your student numbers.

For example, knowing how many students you have had on each course over the last two or three years will allow you to decide which geographical areas or market sectors you want to concentrate your promotional effort on, to make inferences about the long-term trends in your markets which will affect your strategic plans and to make forward predictions which will feed into your forecasts and future budgets.

Bad reasons for collecting statistics:

- You've always done it and it's now part of the system.
- It makes work for people to do.
- You have the computer facility to do it.
- You plan to collate and use them one day, even though you're not sure exactly how.

The worst of both worlds is to collect the information, collate it, and then not do anything much with it. But a lot of schools do exactly this.

Having decided you have good reasons, the next step is to *define the parameters* or dimensions of the information. The more parameters, the more work goes in, the more detail can come out. If you need it, and are really going to use it, fine. Otherwise, keep it simple.

The basic parameters are 1) students and 2) periods, in other words, how many students you have enrolled in a certain period of time. When you build up sets of statistics for a number of periods, you can then make *historical comparisons* to see whether the numbers are going up or down and how fast. These historical comparisons are often only meaningful when considered on an annual basis. If we consider a very basic set of student statistics:

Term	1	2	3
Students	280	340	185

It is difficult to interpret this usefully, except to say that the middle term appears to be the most popular, until we add the statistics for a couple more years:

	Term	1	2	3	Total
Year 1	Students	280	340	180	800
Year 2	Students	265	320	195	780
Year 3	Students	275	310	220	805

Now we can say that the numbers in the middle term are actually declining, numbers in the third term are climbing, while numbers in the first term and overall numbers are more or less static. These trends might suggest you should transfer more resources to term 3 in the next couple of years, and perhaps research into whether students are transferring from term 2 to term 3, and if so why.

Other common parameters are 3) course type, 4) source of booking, and 5) nationality; less commonly, average length of stay, level, age, and sex. The number of parameters is potentially infinite, and as every institution is different, what may be crucial information in one place might be of no interest in another. For example, the drop-out rate for each type of course, the rate of progress through the levels, or the proportion of re-enrolments from former students.

When you include such other parameters, you can make *snapshot comparisons*, to see for example what proportion of your students are direct bookings as opposed to coming through commissionable sources, or how many are in intensive rather than non-intensive courses. The most useful information comes from a combination of these comparisons, so that you can follow the trends in your nationality mix, or breakdown of student numbers by course type, over a period of time. Ideally, you want to be able to anticipate questions you might want to ask in the future: for example, is there a seasonal factor in the proportion of company-sponsored students versus direct bookings?

Parameter 1: students

Unless you have absolutely standard courses of fixed length and intensity, it is convenient to define a basic unit such as student/weeks or group/hours, in order to make the information more meaningful. Obviously, if one student stays for two weeks and another for twenty, you want to be able to reflect that difference in the statistics, and not just count each as one student. The first would count as two student/weeks, and the second as twenty student/weeks (usually abbreviated to 20 StWks or S/W).

Incidentally, if you offer free places for promotional or scholarship purposes, are you going to count them in the statistics? In principle no, since they are not fee-paying, but if the numbers involved are small and it's a bother to count them out, then leave them in.

Parameter 2: period

The period can be weeks, course months (ie four week periods), calendar months, terms, semesters, or other artificial units – don't be afraid to make up a convenient unit if it helps to meet the objectives. You may wish to use different units or different periods for different course types, in order to make comparisons within each course type more accurate (ie you can say precisely how each course type is doing compared to the last period or last year). For example, the statistics for private lessons might be given in student/hours while those for group classes are measured in student/weeks. The gain in low-level precision involves a loss in high-level generalization – you clearly cannot add statistics measured in different units, so cannot produce a single overall indicator, although one way out of this is to average out the typical number of student/hours in a week to convert the student/hours to student/weeks. For example, if you have seventy student/hours of private lessons in one week, and you know the average is ten hours per week, for summary purposes you can count it as seven student/weeks.

Parameter 3: course type

Assuming that you have more than one course type with a significant number of students, you will want to follow the individual trends for these different courses over time. This information will be particularly important in deciding your future strategy (see Section 4, pp 23–30).

Parameter 4: source of booking

Many schools and centres get a large number of their students from one particular source, which may be a parent or sister company, other departments within the same institution, or other schools or colleges with which it has an especially close relationship. It is crucial to analyze this dominance of the major single client, firstly to see exactly how important they are and secondly to ensure that their sheer volume of business is not distorting your overall statistics and concealing other important trends. More generally, where you have several different sources of bookings, such as agency bookings (which are commissionable), direct bookings (which are not), renewals and re-enrolments from former students, block bookings from company clients, and perhaps closed group bookings from other sources such as schools or government agencies, you will probably want to isolate each one in order to identify important trends for planning and marketing purposes.

Parameter 5: nationality

For institutions with a multinational student mix, this obviously enables you to identify your geographical sources of students. You may want to consolidate certain nationalities together into regional or continental groupings to make numbers that are big enough to show significant trends; at the same time, you need to watch out for distinct sub-groups, where within a particular nationality there might be two or more separate markets, according to course type, age, length of stay or time of year.

Interaction of parameters

Very often, it is the combination of these parameters that reveals the most significant information – for example, that most of the direct bookings enrol at the beginning of the academic year but gradually drop out as the year wears on; that there is less market for part-time courses for local students in the summer, or that many South Americans travel in groups in January and February. While statistical techniques such as analysis of variance will isolate such interactions between parameters and the strength of their relationship, unless you have such facilities available on computer you will learn more by sorting through the data by hand, comparing your results against other schools', testing hypotheses and following up hunches.

A more detailed and authentic example of student statistics is given in the appendix (Section 1: Marketing statistics, p 163).

The general point here is that such statistics can yield a lot of information, but also yield a lot of multiple possibilities. 'The result is clearly such-and-such, but the cause might be A, or B or C.' To determine which is the correct cause, and thus exploit the statistical data successfully, you need a lot of outside information as well, such as how other schools are performing and therefore whether they are experiencing the same trends or not.

Clearly, you also need a very good knowledge of all aspects of your own institution, so that you know on a daily basis how things are going and have a sense of intuition for the reasons why, but the more you already know about the internal workings of the institution, the more likely you are to have your own particular ideas about what is right and what is wrong, and will look to the statistics only for confirmation of these. And as with most statistics, if you look hard enough you can usually find the evidence you want to back up almost any argument.

Student records are only the raw material for management planning and decision-making. These statistics have no inherent meaning on their own, but depend largely on the context of the school and the wider local or national context to make them meaningful. For example, for the school in Appendix Section 1 the minute upturn in overall business in 1993 was so small as to be insignificant, but in the light of the previous three years' major loss of business and against a generally reported drop of 10–12 per cent in business in that year, it seems quite an achievement.

Again, these statistics have nothing to do with profit and loss: the school involved may have controlled expenses rigorously and achieved an increased level of profit by deliberately cutting down on unprofitable business, for example by raising prices on courses that were unprofitable. Without knowing the relative prices of each course, and the scale of discounts offered, we are in no position to comment on the wider story.

Summary

RULE 1: Keep it simple!
The more parameters you add, the longer the information takes to collect and process, and the more complex it becomes to interpret.

RULE 2: Integrate the collection of statistics into your other information systems.
In other words, rather than setting up a wholly new and completely separate process to collect and analyze the statistics for marketing and management purposes, see if it is possible to combine it with the existing enrolment system, for example, and the presentation of results with your existing reporting system.

RULE 3: Don't allow data collection to become an end in itself.
This sounds obvious, but it's surprising how easily you can find yourself making extra work out of habit, as the true story on p 23 may illustrate.

• •

True story   *A good servant and a bad master*

A large school in a central European city purchased a computer system at just the wrong time – when they were large and expensive, needed custom-tailored programming, and a couple of years before micro-computers revolutionized the way we store and process information. The system they purchased was a mini computer, which took over a small classroom, required a special ventilation system, and a High Priest to look after it, for which job one of the admin. staff was detached from other duties for training. So far, this story is just bad timing, which can happen to anybody.

The next bit is bad management. The custom-written suite of programs was never finished and never worked properly, largely because the school management kept changing the specifications. It *did* produce useful statistical information, but because of the peculiar nature of the programming, only the High Priest could input the statistical data, and coax out the results. The system was disliked and mistrusted by reception staff, who had to use it to generate invoices, because of its unreliability and complexity and their lack of understanding of it.

Although the idiosyncrasies of the Machine were well recognized and frequently discussed, it was always cheaper to keep on with it than cut the losses and start again. To cut a long story short, for many years the Machine was dictating to management the kind of information they could collect; one quite well-paid member of staff did little else but tend to the Machine; and both Machine and High Priest required each other, in a symbiotic relationship, to justify and maintain their existence.

Finally, the High Priest was made redundant, the Machine was switched off, and the school bought a micro system for less than the cost of the annual service contract on the Machine. Several more micros followed, and each manager and receptionist soon had their own system, on their own desk, under their own control. Using an 'off-the-shelf' database program, the system for collection and manipulation of statistical data continued to evolve, but it didn't matter – the report generator allowed a competent but non-expert computer user to design and try out new reports, without changing the basic data. The system is still in use today.

• •

4   How do you know what direction the school should move in?
How can you develop a strategy and set targets?

> A (...) manager at any stage should endeavour to have a clear view of the future, and the role that he would like his business to play in that future.

> (Harvey-Jones 1988 p 39)

Bear your statement of aims (see Chapter 1) in mind while developing your strategy, but don't let it dictate what you can and can't do. If the opportunities and advantages you want to exploit don't fit with what your statement of aims says, then it probably needs rethinking, and the exercise will result in a useful clarification of your objectives. Formulating strategy should be a continuous process, a continuing dialogue in both the staffroom and the boardroom or backroom.

The five-step approach to strategy formulation

You can carry out this exercise on your own, or with colleagues; at a single session, or over a period of time; as a focused and goal-oriented activity or as a more open-ended opportunity to generate ideas and promote a sense of teamwork at the same time. The most positive long-term results may come from an extended but quite informal meeting held in a relaxed environment, off the premises, preferably not at the end of a normal working day.

| **1** | **External forecast** - an analysis of **P**olitical, **E**conomic, **S**ocial and **T**echnological factors. |

| **2** | **Internal forecast** - an analysis of your **S**trengths, **W**eaknesses, **O**pportunities and **T**hreats. |

| **3** | **Your services** - an objective look at the various services you offer. |

| **4** | **Identify opportunities** - list, but don't evaluate at this stage, as many opportunities as possible that you can identify. |

| **5** | **Evaluate opportunities** - and focus on the competitive advantages that can be exploited from the opportunities. |

Step 1: External forecasts

What are the events and trends taking place in the outside world that may affect the way your institution will develop? It is most unlikely that you can influence these factors. The point here is to recognize them as they are happening and to consider their implications for your institution's future.

These general forecasts may be global, regional, national, or local. Some questions to start off with:

- **What is the political climate in your major market(s)?**
  What changes in government policy could affect your business? (eg tax laws, training funds, legislation on registration or recognition, a more or less favourable climate for pressure groups).
- **What are the major economic trends?**
  Broadly speaking, is business expanding or contracting? Is it confident?
  Is there more international trade or more protectionism?
  Is it easier or harder to send money out/bring money in?
  Is the exchange rate moving, making a currency more or less valuable?
  Is the individual's purchasing power increasing or decreasing?
- **What are the major trends in travel, tourism and leisure?**
  What effects are political and economic factors having?
  Are there more people going to/coming from abroad?
  Is the trend towards package tourism or catering for individuals?
  Are international airfares rising, holding level or falling?

- **What are the major changes in education and training?**
  What are the demographic changes to the pupil/student population?
  Are more young people staying longer in higher education?
  Is boom or recession boosting or cutting company-sponsored training?
- **What technological innovations could become relevant?**
  (eg improved communications leading to a greater need for foreign languages;
  the widespread take-up of foreign-based software and hardware; etc).

Most such general forecasts can only come from other sources, such as newspapers, and may not seem at first sight to have any useful implications for your own strategic review. But at this stage they are all worth listing, along with general predictions that relate to any particular industry or business that you are tied to or are heavily dependent upon.

Step 2: Internal forecasts

How is your institution placed in the local market? Start off by throwing out some specific forecasts for the language-teaching market in your location, looking back over the last five years and forward to the next five:

- What has happened to the ELT provision in the last five years? How has the market changed? What have these changes been in response to?
- Are these changes 'played out' or will they continue?
- What other factors may affect ELT provision in the next five years?
- Is the provision for English language teaching in schools increasing? From what age? Is it meeting the demand from parents, from employers and from the government? If not, how is that demand being met?

Now pull these factors together in lists of your strengths, weaknesses, opportunities and threats. Here are a few ideas:

Strengths:	Weaknesses:
long-established and well-known; generally positive name and image for 'value-for-money'; good location for business clients and access to transport; loyal company clients; high staff morale and positive atmosphere.	high fixed overheads; quite high prices; limited range of courses; defensive attitudes among senior staff which limit innovation; premises need major overhaul, or are perhaps unsuitable for new courses you would like to run; no financial cushion; contract teachers often under-utilized.
Opportunities:	**Threats:**
new markets and clients in particular regions/areas where you have a foothold; develop existing contacts with teachers to exploit gaps in new national syllabuses; new discount formula for existing students to renew/return could be extended further; trial of flexible 'pay-as-you-learn' scheme popular with direct bookings.	small schools starting locally with lower wage costs and smaller overheads; major company clients preferring to employ own teaching staff directly and/or promote self-study; improved state sector provision is making the elementary student a rare species; improved college/university provision is reducing your student market; many more students are being attracted to other countries, eg Australia or the USA.

Step 3: Your services

Consider the various courses and services you offer. List each course type and other service, and for each one, briefly summarize:

- its recent performance;
- its current importance in your range;
- its future potential.

You should include all the major services you offer that are intended to generate income in their own right. Don't include in this analysis services that are not intended to make a profit and are purely ancillary to your main activities (although you can certainly ask if they couldn't become independently profitable, and make a note to list them as new opportunities in step 4 – for example, being a local examination centre, selling a range of student books at a small profit, or offering a language testing consultancy).

It is useful, if harsh, to sum up by placing each product or service in one of these boxes:

	now	**future**
profitable	'cash cow'	'rising star'
unprofitable	'pet'	'dog'

Fig. 2.2 (for more detail on this model, see Dibb 1991 p 562)

Many courses will not fit conveniently into one of these boxes, but slide from one to another; they may be profitable most of the year, but lose money in the low season; or they may have been reliable cash cows until recently, then have lurched into the red, and have been granted a stay of execution to see how they perform over the next year. But the simplistic black-and-white perspective *is* useful; there *are* good reasons for keeping pets, but as the name implies, one's own reasons for keeping them may be governed by emotion rather than reason!

The real benefit of this exercise, therefore, is not to pigeonhole complex services into unrealistically simple categories, but to encourage you to challenge your conventional rationalizations.

Do you have any pets? Why? A former cash cow that you're perhaps too attached to? Something you're convinced will become a rising star? A loss-leader you need to keep up to maintain your claim that ...? Seen in black and white (often the best perspective!), you need a convincing reason for keeping on with something that is not profitable now and may not be in the future.

How sure can you be that a particular pet is going to become a rising star rather than a dog? If this turns out to be wrong, when is the right time to cut the losses and drop it? Before you cut anything, is there really no way to improve its efficiency so that the dog becomes a minor cash cow (for example, improving staff utilization, raising the minimum number of students required to run a class, asking for payment in full further in advance and then chasing it)?

● ●

True stories *Pigeonholes*

Some real examples of a course of each kind:

The cash cow
The general intensive course that has been the main course offered longer than anyone can remember. I wonder if it is really as lucrative as we think, or whether everything else is now so structured around it that it just *appears* to be very profitable?

The rising star
The language travel package that includes parties, barbecues, discos, special outings arranged to order to fulfil individual ambitions, and finally a weekend in Paris: Versailles on Friday, Paris tour and shopping on Saturday and Eurodisney on Sunday. There is also a teaching component.

The pet
The teachers' course was designed to meet the needs of non-native-speaker teachers who are already fully qualified and experienced and who want an opportunity to meet, to talk, to exchange views and experiences, and in theory to improve their own language awareness and keep up-to-date with methodology. In practice, not only is the course unteachable because they *won't* sit still and listen, let alone keep to the point for five minutes, it is also unprofitable because although there always seems to be plenty of demand, somehow it never translates into firm bookings when needed.

The dog
This was the way the one-to-one courses looked as the economy entered a prolonged recession. They were individually profitable as long as the volume was enough to justify all the individual scheduling time and attention spent on them; but when the numbers dropped, there were increasing gaps in the teaching schedules of the experienced and therefore highly paid teachers whom the one-to-one clients demanded, and these gaps could not be filled by regular classes. The question was, 'Is it worth hanging on to the one-to-one programme, knowing it is really going to lose money, so as to be ready to pick up the new business as soon as the economy improves?' With the great benefit of hindsight, the answer was 'no' – even when the recovery started, the one-to-one programme continued to lose money for a long time. It should have been axed when the problem was first spotted.

● ●

Ideally, a school should have a mixed portfolio of courses and services: some future stars that will ensure future well-being, and some cash cows generating the funds needed for that future growth. In ELT, the investment required for rising stars is usually in the areas of market research, course development and promotion. Which of the possibilities will need the least funds to lift it into a rising star? Which could be the most successful?

TIP It can be useful at this stage to invite a competitor in! The books usually say, 'now it's time to take an objective look at the various products and services you offer ...'. This is a virtual impossibility: it is difficult to be objective about what you are doing, particularly when it is a complex network of interdependent services. Think of a competitor whom you trust but who in some way has a different perspective, and preferably is not a direct competitor, who in other words is not offering exactly the same services as you in the same locality. At the same time it should be someone who knows all aspects of the business well enough to take a really dispassionate view of what you're doing. One positive way to arrange this is on an exchange basis, and it must be understood that the visitor can ask any questions and challenge any assumptions. She or he must be prepared to play 'the Devil's advocate' by taking nothing for granted and questioning every cherished belief.

Step 4: Identify opportunities

List, but don't evaluate at this stage, as many opportunities as possible that you can identify from a review of:

- existing courses
  We could extend/adapt/make more flexible _____ .
- new courses
  We could run a _____ .
- new activities
  Since we're located in an area that _____
  why not _____ .
- new markets
  We've never tried running courses for _____ .
- new opportunities
  How can we exploit the recent development of _____?
- new liaisons
  Let's approach _____ to suggest a joint programme
  to develop and sell a course for _____ .
- human resources
  Since we have staff with _____ experience,
  why don't we _____ .
- other resources
  Could we let any of our classrooms out to _____ ?

If you're working on this collectively, you could use this as a questionnaire to be filled in by each person, then pool the ideas.

True story   *On the sixth day*

A town-centre school started a new weekend course, on Saturday mornings. It seemed a huge departure, but hourly-paid teachers were always keen to do a couple of hours extra, and the administrative staff were willing to staff it on a rota basis, for time off in lieu during the week rather than extra pay; so for no extra cost, there was an increased utilization of premises and resources that were otherwise completely unused for two days out of seven. And, incidentally, the Saturday morning programme was judged by both staff and students to be successful: unlike the more usual 'end-of-the-day' fatigue, they felt refreshed and relaxed, with most of the weekend to come, which created a marvellous atmosphere.

Step 5: Evaluate opportunities

Focus on the competitive advantages that can be exploited from the opportunities. If this is a think-tank exercise rather than a decision-making one, it may still be useful to proceed as if you are formulating a real-life survival plan, which means:

1 Select the opportunities for action.
2 Formulate the strategic plan.
3 Set targets and define time scales for each part of the plan.

Why set targets?

1 To evaluate each course or service as it goes along, not wait until too late to find out it's not working.
2 To be able to compare more generally how the various courses or services are doing, so that you can switch sales resources, for example, from intensive courses to part-time courses or from company-sponsored students to direct bookings; and so that at the end of the year or period you have an objective criterion against which to measure success or failure.
3 Motivation and team-building. Targets give people something to aim for and if taken seriously they promote discussion about how to get there. The targets should be *high* enough to stretch people, they need to be *achievable* to be taken seriously, and they must be *negotiated* with the people concerned to have any real value.
4 Targets interpret the institution's objectives in everyday terms. Without them, there is a major risk that the statement of aims (see Chapter 1) will remain only an expression of good intentions.

What sort of targets?

Targets may be expressed in terms of sales income, student numbers (or student/weeks) or class size averages (occupancy rate) for a particular course, ie numerical targets; or they can be expressed in terms of non-numerical objectives, such as the development of new courses; the introduction of an appraisal system; specific improvements to premises, furnishing or equipment.

In all cases, it is crucial that the target has a clear date and is 'transparently checkable', so that it is easily evident whether or not it has been achieved. It also needs to be made clear who is responsible for each target; they may be collective or they may be individual, in which case you can elaborate and evaluate them as individual goals in your appraisal system.

Finally, what happens when the targets are reached or are not reached? It's important to specify this. Does the course get axed or restructured, or are staff merely going to say 'The target was unrealistic,' which undermines the whole exercise?

5 What is a realistic time scale for course development?

The strategy formulation process above should have identified where you want to go, and with what degree of urgency. The next step is to translate these goals into a detailed and realistic timetable to get there. Here is a checklist for the development of a new course.

1 Identify the stages. For example:

- detailed market research;
- detailed planning including detailed costing;
- arranging finance;
- finding teaching premises or accommodation;
- recruiting and/or training staff;
- writing syllabuses and course planning;
- writing materials and/or manuals;
- preparing promotional materials;
- promotion and sales;
- getting validation.

2 Identify the people involved in each stage.

3 Identify the major constraints (time, money, validation, premises, resources, etc), and outline how and when these constraints can be satisfied.

4 Identify which stages are dependent on others and must be sequential, ie have to be completed in a particular order; and which stages are independent, and can be carried out whenever convenient.

5 Put a maximum and minimum time limit on each stage.

6 Draw up a calendar with actual target dates, allowing a little extra time at each stage for slippage. If you are working to a particular seasonal business or academic calendar *(we need to have this course ready by next summer),* it may be worth doing this step backwards, ie setting the date for the last stage first, then the one before it, and so on.

Having got some idea of what you want to do, how quickly is it realistic to be able to do it? The short answer is: one year. The longer answer, of course, is 'it depends':

Course design

This can take anywhere from one to six months, depending on how much time and concentrated effort you can put into it at one time.

Promotion

- If you want to include the new course in your general brochure, you will want to plan it in time for your next reprint, so that it will become generally known in good time.
- If you are going to produce a separate brochure, flyer or other promotional material, you will need at least two to three months to produce it and get it to the right people.
- If you are going to work through agents, you will need time to get the information to them: probably two or three months; and plenty of time for them to sell it on to their customers: another six to nine months; altogether, eight to twelve months. A lot of the fine detail of the course design can obviously be added when the promotional campaign is already under way, but you must clearly have made all the major decisions before you can begin the promotion. No one is going to buy something that appears ill-thought-through or only half finished.

• •

True story   *City kids*

A medium-sized language school in the centre of a large town saw an opportunity for a children's course aimed at ten to fifteen-year-olds to complement its 16+ general course. Market research among their adult students and their competitors suggested that demand was growing in this area and that the project was worth pursuing.

The school was able to use its existing premises, which were under-utilized in the afternoons when the middle and secondary schools came out. The development was entirely in-house – a senior teacher was put in charge of the project, and was sent on a training course for teaching children.

As the aim of the course was to complement what many people, especially parents, felt to be the major gaps in the national syllabuses (fluency and communication activities) there was no need for a major syllabus-writing project, and suitable teaching materials were readily available (one publisher donated class sets). The whole project took only six months to get off the ground, and it was logically scheduled to fit in with the start of the new academic year.

Generally, it has been a reasonable success, but looking back, four points stand out:

1 Few people actually live in the immediate area, and while there are a lot of adults going to and from work and college, most children have to travel or be brought there; parking is not easy. The course has therefore been more successful in recruiting older children (fourteen or fifteen years) who can get there on their own.

2 Teenagers are very sensitive to differences of age, especially coming from a rigidly age-graded state system. The juniors therefore have to be allocated to classes as much by age as by actual language level, which can lead to multi-ability classes, which in turn are more difficult for inexperienced teachers. By the same token, the materials chosen cannot be directly related in any way to the books in use in the state sector. Considerable experience is needed, and has now been built up, in placing students and choosing materials.

3 Planning for the new course to start with the new academic year was an assumption that was in hindsight unnecessary. Students now can, and do, join at any time of year; and the school is now planning short, intensive summer holiday courses for juniors.

4 Younger children, especially, are naturally noisy. There is a need to segregate children from adult students, eg during breaks.

● ●

6 How do you promote the school and its courses?

The raw materials that you bring to this stage are:

- Your statement of aims – your general objectives and raison d'être; this should crystallize your identity, which will help define the style and image you want to project.
- The strategic plan (Section 4, pp 23–30) – your specific goals.
- The time scale (Section 5, pp 30–1) for the achievement of those goals.
- Your existing promotional materials (depending on whether you want to present a gentle continuity or a striking new departure).

Word of mouth

Before getting involved in detailed discussions of materials, remember the easily forgotten but obvious rule: The best form of advertising is personal recommendation ('word of mouth').

> The idea of people making recommendations to other people is so familiar to us that it often takes a big stretch of the imagination to understand what a significant factor it can be in improving the profitability of your business. Most business owners have no idea just how powerful this tool is because they don't know how to use it efficiently. Yet ask yourself how many of the interesting people you have met, places you have visited, and more to the point, high quality small businesses with whom you have had positive relationships, have come to you from friends caring enough to tell you about them.

(Phillips and Rasberry 1986 p 1)

Important points to remember about 'word of mouth':

- It can be negative just as easily as positive: in fact, an unhappy customer tells a lot more people about their experience than a happy one.
- It doesn't have to be first-hand – it may well be second or third-hand, but still quite valid ('My brother/colleague/friend went to the X School of English, and he said ...').
- It may be based on unpredictable criteria, such as personal likes and dislikes; or it may be based on an objective overall view. You do not know and will usually never find out: every and any aspect of your operation can lead to further business, or to loss of it. You therefore need to adopt a 'total quality approach' which is flexible enough to examine every aspect.
- You *can*, however, try to establish how many students come through personal recommendation, and to find out whether they in turn will recommend you to others, and if so what aspects they particularly liked.

A simple checklist for using 'word of mouth':

1 Are you personally happy with every major aspect of your operation? If not, don't deliberately try to promote personal recommendations: if you aren't happy, the chances are others won't be either. Solve the problems first, or at the very least, show that the organization is aware of them and has plans underway to solve them.

2 Do you have built-in but flexible mechanisms for finding out what your students think of the school, and are likely to say to others? For example, student committees and student questionnaires (see Section 2, pp 16–17); informal but regular conversation between staff and students before, between or after lessons; a suggestions box or system for all staff and students.

3 Is internal communication good? If a student makes a casual comment to a member of staff about, for example, the cleanliness of the premises or the punctuality of their teacher, can you be sure that it will be passed on and dealt with? If not, what steps can you take to improve this communication?

4 Is there any convenient opportunity when you could talk to one student at a time in greater depth, over a period of time, to gain their confidence and find out what they really think, and how their reactions to the service they are getting change over time? This is a question about client-focus: seeing things as far as you can from their point of view, not yours.

5 To a casual visitor, eg someone just phoning or dropping in to get information, is the atmosphere welcoming? How long does it take to get straightforward answers to information questions? Do the 'front-line' staff know enough about your courses to be able to talk about them honestly and knowledgeably?

6 Do the staff seem to enjoy working there?

7 Are your courses at least above average standard?

8 When there is a problem or a complaint, do you deal with it in a way that inspires confidence, and may actually win a recommendation?

General types of publicity		
	Advantages	**Disadvantages**
Advertising	Mass exposure Effective for quick promotion You have complete control over form and content	Expensive, especially internationally Difficult to focus unless you identify a particular group with its own medium, eg a magazine for English teachers May be a language and 'cultural style' barrier If abroad, do you give your contact details, or a local agent's?
Visits	Can be carefully targeted to spend just the time and money you want to visit just the people you want	Time-consuming Can take a couple of weeks just to co-ordinate seeing half a dozen people in the same town
Exhibitions	A good way to meet a lot of people in a short time who are interested in language learning and courses	Often very costly, especially when you include daily expenses May be a lot of time wasters who have no real intention of buying Very tiring!
Press coverage	Cheap, if not free!	Usually difficult to get, and impossible to control what is said; sensationalism of any kind is unlikely to help
Educational talks, tours and seminars	Good for the image of the organization	The benefits are uncertain and long-term, if they exist at all

Promotional materials

When planning and reviewing your promotional materials, it may be useful to think through your range of existing materials in terms of *style, form* and *content*. The following is a short checklist for each type of material:

- COST, including cost of subsequent reprints: what is the longest sensible print run that won't leave you with boxes of out-of-date and unused brochures in years to come?
- EASILY ALTERABLE – in case you want to add or delete bits. Is it better to include information that is likely to change, eg dates and fees, on a separate insert that is easily and cheaply revised?
- TARGET AUDIENCE – focused on agents, companies, individuals or very general?
- METHOD AND COST OF DISTRIBUTION (post can add substantially, especially overseas);
- TECHNICAL FORMAT (eg size for printing, format for video, slides);
- LANGUAGE VERSIONS.

Types of promotional material (for brochures, see Section 7)		
	Advantages	**Disadvantages**
Flyers and leaflets	Cheap to produce, so can be given away freely Can be quickly updated or translated	Not usually very attractive or substantial
Posters	Good for showing photos and giving a 'feel' Continue to be effective once they're on display	May be difficult to arrange display in suitable locations
Video	A very powerful medium once in the right hands (eg of a good agent)	Very expensive to produce (allow £1000–£2000 per minute)
Photos and slides	Much cheaper to produce, and easier to update than video Easy to change selection to reflect changes in market strategy	You have little or no control over how your visuals are used. Watch out for agents using your best pictures to illustrate a competitor's text!
Personal testimonials and references	Are very credible, and valuable particularly in less common languages	Can be difficult to get them, and then difficult for you to check what has been said
Tangible freebies (pens, calendars, key-rings, T-shirts, etc – even lists of irregular verbs!)	A well-chosen gift creates a lasting impression	Something obviously cheap or tacky may give the wrong image
Free samples (free courses, scholarships, raffled places, etc)	A good product sells itself – a free place or incentive is a direct expression of confidence in your services	Despite apparently minimal cost, they can work out expensive in the long run

7   How do you design a new brochure?

The brochure is really just of one of many promotional materials used by schools, so strictly speaking it belongs in the previous section; but it is so important, for some schools virtually their only promotional material, that it deserves its own section.

The Brochure Recipe

——— *Preparation time* ———
one to three months

——————— *Ingredients* ———————
your statement of aims
your strategic plan
your existing and recent brochures
your closest competitors' brochures
other brochures you particularly like and dislike
a lot of photographs and/or drawings
a graphic designer (optional but recommended)

——————————————— *Method* ———————————————

1 Decide the TARGET (*who it's for*) and the MESSAGE (*what it's supposed to tell them*). Be as specific as possible – if your honest answer is 'All things for all people,' your brochure will reflect just that. If you can, consult a graphic designer at an early stage, and use him or her as a sounding board for your ideas as well as a source of professional advice.

2 Noting constraints such as likely print run, shelf life, postage costs and language versions, decide what options of format (size, colour, number of pages) are open to you. Look at other brochures; identify why you like or dislike particular features in yours, your competitors', or others'.

3 Start playing around with different layouts: which bit of the message should go where? What should the cover say, in terms of visual impact? What is the general effect you want the brochure to have? Several people can usefully contribute at this stage.

4 Sit down and write the text, perhaps several different drafts. Type or print them, make several copies, start cutting and pasting, on screen or literally with a pair of scissors, moving text and pictures around the dummy pages. Involve just one or two people at this stage.

5 Ask for different opinions, and listen to them, but don't feel you have to act on every one! Now go through the whole thing again on your own, checking that every page and every section reflects the target and message you identified. You should now definitely consult a graphic designer to add an extra touch of class to the appearance.

6 Get two or preferably three estimates; negotiate, bargain hard. Ask to see samples of work if you don't know the designer already. Ask for recommendations from friends and colleagues. Be specific about delivery dates.

8   How do you decide the fees for next year?

Don't just take your current prices and add X per cent for inflation.
Do be methodical about it; it is a rare opportunity to re-align yourself in the market. Here is a suggested procedure:

Step 1

Your statement of aims (Chapter 1, pp 9–11) and your strategic plan (Chapter 2, pp 23–30) will tell you the direction you want to be moving in. Specifically, you need to review or decide where you want to position your school in terms of price in the particular markets that you have targeted. You need as objective an assessment as possible of whether these markets are expanding or contracting.

Do you have a strong enough reputation, and plenty of demand, to push the price up a bit? Do you want to position your school higher up the market? Or do you feel that you need to increase numbers by offering the same service at lower prices? Can you increase business, or attract potential students away from competitors, by keeping prices down, with tight cost control?

TIP 'Pruning roses is quicker than cultivating new ones, yet may encourage vigorous growth.' The quickest way to make a profit is by cutting costs, not by increasing income. Cutting costs is painful, but you can do it immediately. Increasing income takes time, hard work and a bit of luck.

Step 2

Research the current prices of the competitors a) offering the kind of courses that you are offering or aiming towards; b) who are geographically close to you; and c) who are best represented in the countries where you would like to increase student recruitment. It is often difficult to make exact comparisons, but try to draw up a comparative price table, making allowances for differences as far as possible (eg booking or registration fees, class size, number of lessons, etc).

Step 3

Make an estimate of the likely increase in your costs over the next year. This will involve a general forecast of inflation, as well as specific forecasts of the likely changes in your major expenses, namely salaries, premises, materials, taxes and utilities. Although some are impossible to predict, others may be following a general trend or previous agreement (eg inflation-indexing of salaries and long-term rent agreements).

Step 4

Using the information from steps 1, 2 and 3 above, work out what is the optimal price for your courses. Now create a budget spreadsheet for next year, if you have not already done so. Feed in the optimal figures and realistic estimates of the number of students or student/weeks you can reasonably expect at those prices, and see what the proverbial 'bottom line' is. You will probably need to repeat this stage many times; if so, print out and keep a copy of each, noting the date and time and the particular variables that you were experimenting with.

Chapter 3 Selling

Introduction

Selling is the process of getting someone to buy what you are offering – in this case, language courses at your school. Although you may occasionally be able to interest people who had not already been thinking of buying a language course (in the same way that we might buy an ice cream on the spur of the moment, because there happens to be vendor in the right place at the right time), almost always you are dealing with people who have already made a decision and are 'shopping around'. In other words, you are competing with other schools for their business.

What selling is not:

- finding out what people want and will buy (this is marketing);
- matching up what you offer with what people want (course design);
- telling people who you are and what you offer (promotion and publicity).

Some marketing and promotional activities may lead directly to sales, and some sales activities also have a promotional effect; but in general you must have completed these other stages before you can begin to sell. Selling is successful only when you reach agreement and students ultimately attend your school in return for fees paid.

1 What are you selling?

1 Courses

You made decisions about the exact nature of your courses at the strategic planning and course development stages (see Chapter 2, Section 4 and Section 5). For example:

- year-round general English – full-time and part-time;
- vacation courses – adult residential/non-residential;
- vacation courses – junior (12-18) residential/non-residential;
- courses for children (under 12);
- executive/very intensive and one-to-one courses;
- specific courses (ESP) – business, technical, academic English, etc;
- courses for teachers.

While the course format itself is pre-determined, you need to keep some flexibility to present it in the way that you judge most suits clients' needs or arouses their interest.

2 The experience

Look at it from the student's point of view. Think about it for a minute, and speculate on what it might be like: how you would spend your time, what aspects you would most enjoy.

Now ask yourself how much of the anticipation is for the course, and how much for other possible pleasures – leisure, people, a break from your usual job and home routine, good food and drink, new sights, sunshine, sports, etc.

The point is that it is easy to think that what you are selling is the language course. However, in fact what the student is buying is not just the course, but the school, the town/region/country, and the whole experience.

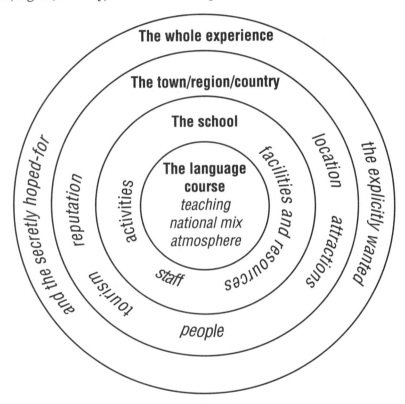

Fig. 3.1: What is the student buying?

You can't afford to be selling just the course when the student is buying the other things as well.

The school selling to local students is obviously unable to sell the physical environment of the other culture directly, but it can still evoke it indirectly by deliberately creating 'a small corner of a foreign country' and encouraging students to enjoy it vicariously. Crude manifestations of this are flags, travel posters, cut-out British policemen and phone boxes. More sophisticated exponents can involve style of furnishing as well as decor; use of target language outside classes as well as inside (make the building a target-language zone, not just the classroom); regular lectures and seminars; displays/loan of books, magazines, newspapers, and cassettes; (satellite) TV or video in lounges and waiting areas etc.

3 Your special feature

In a market where there is a lot of competition offering more or less similar courses, the potential client can be forgiven for saying 'Well, what's different about your school? Why should I choose yours from the two hundred others that offer the same course?'

The answer is to have something special about your school or programme that distinguishes you from the competition and gives the client something to remember you by.

- It might be the building or its location; the group size or nationality mix; the level of equipment or furnishing, or free access to a self-study centre or other special facilities at any time.
- It might be an extra component to the programme – arranging free conversation exchange; extra lessons or 'language workshops'; weekly lunch with the teacher; an opportunity for the student to meet local people with the same interests; a big night out; a post-course follow-up package of self-teaching materials, or whatever.
- It might be a 'no-quibble' money-back guarantee if the student fails to reach a specified target level, or is unhappy with the course.
- It might be subliminal messages of genuine respect and caring for the individual as a real person, not just as a paying customer.
- It might be something as simple as free coffee and biscuits.
- It might be arranging for non-teaching staff to mix with students in breaks on a regular or irregular basis.
- It might be any combination of these. It doesn't have to be the same all the time. Obviously, there are certain features that you can't change or wouldn't want to, but in other cases you can vary the special feature according to the individual. You plan the courses and the programmes as carefully as you can, but you leave a degree of flexibility so that it is always possible to personalize it.
- You might have up your sleeve a list of the kind of features mentioned above. You wouldn't offer all of them all of the time for any one client. Most of them might have no special value; your aim should be to be able to offer something special to each individual. What you want is for them to say 'I like the sound of that and I want it for myself/for my students.'
- Crucially and intangibly, it is a feeling that there is something special about the place. The staff enjoy working there, feel committed to it, and are constantly on the lookout for ways to help clients, not just as grand gestures but as spontaneous acts of friendship and service. This is the total quality approach where staff are fully involved in and committed to an institution; in that sense, they own it and what's happening in it.

In summary, real selling is as much about listening as about talking – finding out about the person you are talking to and tailoring what you are offering, in what is perhaps a small but significant way, to meet their needs or wishes.

2   Who are you selling to?

Sometimes you are selling directly to the individual who will become a student at your school, either at a distance – by brochure, by telephone, by correspondence; or face-to-face – for example, at exhibitions and language fairs in different countries. In such cases, the same person is both the student taking the course and the client paying for it.

At other times, however, you sell through intermediaries – 'go-betweens' of one kind or another: agents (and sub-agents); company training departments; Chambers of Commerce and similar organizations; government ministries and embassies; teachers; parents; other sponsors.

We are using the word 'client' to cover all these people, including direct bookings, teachers and parents, as well as agents and other 'go-betweens'.

In face-to-face meetings, a major influence on what the client agrees to buy is you. Often, the most visible aspect of the school and the course is you. If you are operating in a culture that is new to you, you may find it useful to seek some basic operating tips: should you sell yourself hard? Should you come straight to the point? Should you push people for commitments? Should you avoid any possible expression of disagreement? Because of the diversity of cultures, it is impossible to generalize about such behaviour, except to say be open, be honest, be flexible as far as you can.

When you sell different types of course, you are aiming at different people or groups of people, as shown in the table below:

	Direct to student	Agents	Companies	Chambers of Commerce	Teachers	Parents
General English	☆☆☆	☆☆☆	☆☆☆		☆	☆☆
Adult vacation	☆☆☆	☆☆☆		☆	☆	☆☆☆
Junior vacation		☆☆☆		☆	☆☆☆	☆☆☆
Children		☆☆			☆☆☆	☆☆☆
Executive/ one-to-one	☆	☆☆	☆☆☆	☆☆		
ESP	☆	☆☆	☆☆☆	☆☆☆	☆	

Key: The more stars, the better! This table can only be very general: which kind of client buys which kind of course varies a lot from country to country, as does the proportion of learners wanting to book direct rather than going through an agent.

Fig. 3.2: Who buys what?

Here is some more detail on each kind of client:

Direct clients

Most direct clients choose the general and vacation courses. Having learned about a school from different possible sources, potential students will usually approach a number of schools directly and ask for more information; perhaps by phone, possibly in person, most likely by post. Direct bookings are 'good for business' in that the client pays the full price (you are not paying commission), and the client usually pays in full in advance, though there is more administrative work for the school involved in processing the payment and registration details for one individual than for a member of a group. You may, however, decide to give a discount for:

- early payment of course fees in full;
- a long booking or re-enrolment;
- a low-season booking;
- a booking from someone you think may influence others;
- a friend or relative of a former student.

Direct clients are the best source of personal recommendations (see Chapter 2, Section 6, pp 32–3); it may be worth offering them a discount or other incentive for return visits, or for any further direct bookings they introduce (family, friends, colleagues).

Agents

Agents are characteristic of the language travel business, where the students travel to a native-speaker country to learn the language where it is spoken. This section is therefore largely aimed at such schools. By contrast, schools selling to local students, who do not travel to another country, do not usually use agents because there is no need for a local representative when the school and the student are already in the same town. However, there are still a number of ways in which people in different positions effectively act as recruiting agents for local schools in return for some form of benefit.

Agents sell all kinds of courses, but most specialize in one or two types, eg junior vacation or adult general and specialist English. They are the main source of bookings for many schools located in native-speaker countries.

Sometimes agents sell only the courses. More often, they also add other elements to make up a full 'package': components such as travel, insurance, and the services of a representative are usually included in the price of a holiday course, and may be offered as optional extras on other courses. Some agents are also travel agents, in the regular sense, and in this case the language travel will be only one of a range of packages they offer aimed at different groups (juniors, students, holiday-makers, etc). Such agents may well offer courses at many different schools, and not be particularly bothered which school a student chooses. Other agents specialize in language travel, and hand-pick a much more limited selection of schools on the basis of geographical distribution and range of course types; they tend to have a more personal knowledge of the courses offered, and therefore to steer students towards one they feel is more suitable.

Agents typically work on a fixed commission basis; they take a percentage of the tuition fees paid by students who book through them. The commission rate is most commonly between 10 and 20 per cent. The agent usually collects the full price (gross fee) from the client or sponsor and deducts the commission before passing the remainder (net fee) on to the school; less often, the sponsor will pay the school directly, with the commission then being passed back to the agent.

Variations of this are:

- **a sliding commission scale**, where the size of the commission increases the more students the agent sends.
- **commission on package**, where the commission is calculated as a percentage of the total price of the components the agent is buying from the school – tuition, accommodation, activities, etc. The tuition element on holiday courses is often a relatively small proportion – perhaps only one-third – of the total cost, and if it is not offered as an option separately from the rest of the package, it would be artificial to calculate commission on it alone.
- **a mixture of commission and a contribution to costs** (eg for the promotion by the agent of your school, or several schools who are between them offering a range of courses or course locations).
- **net prices**. The school quotes the fixed price it wishes to receive for the course from the agent, who then add their own costs for administration, promotion, profit margin, etc to determine the final selling price. This means that the school has little or no control over the selling price. This is a situation to be avoided if you are going to have students from two or more sources in the same country at the same time, who may compare prices. In fact, discrepancies are usually more apparent than real, and are due to differences in other added-in costs such as airline flights.

Net prices are typically quoted for a group rather than an individual, and/or for a special course package prepared to a client's specific requirements rather than an 'off-the-shelf' course out of the brochure. Such a quotation would be phrased as 'The net price for these specifications: A) ... B) ... C) ... etc will be £XXX for a group of minimum ten participants.'

Questions to ask a new agent you are considering working with:

- HOW LONG have they been established? If not long, what is their background?
- HOW MANY students did they send last year on which types of course?
- WHICH other schools does the agent work with? Are they accredited? Are they close competitors? (Do you want to appear in the same brochure?)
- WHY does the agent want a new/different school to work with?
- WHAT are their terms of payment?

If you are in any doubt, and you know one or two of the other schools they work with, ring them informally to ask for a 'reference' for the agent.

Some agents distribute the brochures of the schools they work with; they may ask for a special version printed with their own name, address and logo. Other agents produce their own brochures, which may either be exclusive to your school or offer courses at a range of schools. It is not unusual for agents in such cases to ask the schools who will be featured for a contribution towards the cost of producing the brochure. In either case, a trial period of perhaps a year might be worth considering, before you commit any great sum of money, to see if there is a genuine ability to 'deliver the goods'.

Chambers of Commerce

There are many organizations which are not agencies but which are involved in advising and informing local enquirers about language courses: we are using 'Chambers of Commerce' as a convenient label to represent all of them, although the Chambers are only one type of many. Typically, such organizations:

- have some official or semi-official status;
- work on a subscription rather than a commission system;
- invite a certain number of schools to join their information service, and to pay a fixed annual subscription;
- select the schools to offer a range of services, in terms of geographical distribution, course type, price and so on;
- on receiving an enquiry, pick the two or three schools on their list that most closely match the enquirer's specifications, and leave it to the enquirer to decide which school they will book, if any.

Companies

For convenience, this section includes ministries, embassies and official bodies of any country.

Like direct bookings, companies do not charge commission and pay you directly; but they are like agents in that they often have considerable purchasing power and are in a strong financial position, so can afford to beat your prices down in the knowledge that other schools will accept if you don't.

Training managers tend to be conservative in their choice of schools – having set up a good relationship with a school (often on a personal basis), and having established with that school the procedure they expect to be followed, they will stick with it until and unless there is a serious complaint or they have a substantial requirement that the school is unable to satisfy.

It is important to get terms of payment in writing – often it's the biggest and best-known household names who are the slowest to pay, not through poverty or reluctance, just through large-scale bureaucratic machinery. This can also be the case with government and official bodies.

It is also important to find out exactly what a company wants in the way of a report, attendance record, or end-of-course certificate. The efficient completion of this documentation will be of the highest priority for the company. As this may be the greatest extent of your communication with the company apart from with the training department, it will contribute a lot to their judgement of your school; it may also be a requirement before the outstanding fees can be settled.

Remember that in some companies there may be several departments with some responsibility for buying English language training services. This is particularly true of large companies based on several sites or composed of different subsidiaries. If you have existing business with or a good contact in a company, it is worth asking if there are other departments or sections other than the main training department organizing or arranging courses. If there are, get in touch with them using your existing contact as a reference.

Teachers

In some countries, teachers provide the majority of juniors and children for holiday courses. They recruit students from their own schools, or other local schools in their town or region, and either do a deal with a local agent (for whom they in effect act as sub-agents) or may approach schools directly to negotiate terms for their group. They then usually accompany the group on the course, acting as group leaders to deal with any welfare and disciplinary problems. They may themselves welcome the opportunity to attend a suitable course; or they may prefer to have some free time while their group are in lessons.

Terms are normally an agreed commission plus a free place for so many students – for example, one free place for each twelve or fifteen paying students. This free place may be taken by the teacher in the form of a free course, or by another student whose fee adds to the teacher's income.

For the teachers themselves, special courses designed for non-native-speaker teachers are increasingly popular. Such courses are neither purely teacher-training nor general English, but a mixture of both, called for example 'Language improvement for teachers' or 'Language awareness', and perhaps offering options on 'Communicative techniques' or 'Contemporary culture'.

Teachers, particularly teachers of English, are often asked by parents and others which school they recommend, in the belief that they know about courses for adults as well as courses for juniors and children. They are therefore a good source of personal recommendation, and well worth offering a permanent commission arrangement.

Parents

As well as children and juniors, a lot of students in the sixteen to twenty-two age range on adult vacation courses are also sponsored by their parents.

Particularly if they have been on a similar course themselves, parents will be happy to book direct for older children aged fourteen to eighteen – usually called 'juniors' – rather than booking through a large programme being organized by a teacher or an agency.

Parents of younger children aged ten to thirteen naturally prefer them to travel in the security of a larger group, so they will tend to come with school parties. This is preferable for the language school, as the agent/teacher then shares the responsibility for welfare, and reassures the anxious parent that all really is well with junior.

The purpose of this section has been to clarify who you're aiming at. You need now to think about how you're going to make contact with them.

3 How do you make contact?

There are a number of different kinds of 'sales opportunity', each one more or less appropriate for making contact with the clients you want. Broadly speaking, they are:

- word of mouth and re-enrolments;
- agents' workshops (in a native-speaker, regional or local country);
- conferences and seminars;
- exhibitions and fairs;
- mailing (remote personal contact including phone, fax);
- visits.

This table shows which sales opportunities are best for making contact with which kinds of client:

	Word of mouth	Workshops	Fairs	Conferences	Mailing	Visits
Direct	☆☆☆		☆☆☆	☆☆		
Agents	☆☆☆	☆☆☆	☆☆	☆	☆☆☆	☆☆☆
Chambers	☆☆		☆		☆☆☆	☆☆☆
Companies	☆☆		☆☆		☆☆	☆☆☆
Teachers	☆☆		☆☆☆	☆☆☆	☆☆	
Parents	☆☆☆		☆☆☆			

Fig. 3.3: Making contact with potential clients

Let's look at each of these in more detail.

Word of mouth

Personal recommendation was discussed in Chapter 2, Section 6, pp 32–3. It's important to put it top of the 'How do you make contact?' list, because when it works for you, it's free, it's effective and it's a sign of client satisfaction.

It works when you run such a good school that people (companies, agents and teachers as well as individuals) contact you unsolicited, on the basis of a personal recommendation from someone else whose opinion they respect. The best way to sell anything is to make it so good it sells itself, by reputation, by word of mouth, by personal recommendation.

How do you do that with a language course? Is a language course a service? Is it leisure? Is it training? Whatever it is, it is intangible – the thing you are paying money for is not a thing at all. It is the learning that takes place as a result of the teaching, and the management that facilitates the learning and teaching, and the other hidden activities that support the school: accounts, reception, cleaning, etc. All these are people-based. The relatively small areas of things – physical premises, teaching resources – are important, and can contribute to successful learning, but are not nearly as important as the positive atmosphere that is created by people really working together towards a common goal with a shared commitment to achieving the best possible quality of service. Quality sells itself; in this sense, everybody is a salesperson.

Between half and three-quarters of your income is probably spent on salaries. Can you afford – literally – to have anyone working for you or with you who is not working for total quality?

Re-enrolments

Re-enrolments figure here because they are really the same as a personal recommendation – a client is so pleased with their course that they decide to come back (re-enrolment) or stay longer than originally intended (renewal). For convenience, these are treated below as the same thing. You may not wish to go as far as the chains of schools whose sales managers can double or treble their basic salaries by achieving and maintaining high re-enrolment rates: but you cannot afford to ignore the fact that if your school and your colleagues are doing a good job, then you should have a large number of happy repeat customers on your premises.

Techniques for encouraging re-enrolment:

Put a simple and discreet notice in each classroom, perhaps on permanent display, perhaps towards the end of a particular course:

> *Would you like to re-enrol?*
>
> *Do you want to take the Cambridge or TOEFL preparation course?*
>
> *Contact the main reception desk*
>
> or *ask your teacher*
>
> or *see your training manager for details.*

Using either a computer or a manual record system, keep a check of which students' courses are coming to an end. Approach them to find out how they feel about the course, what their future plans are and whether there is a possibility of re-enrolment.

You may want to have a fixed, printed price discount system for re-enrolments; or you may prefer to keep the flexibility of being able to offer a bigger or smaller discount according to the individual's means, how easily you can accommodate their re-enrolment wishes, and their desired further length of stay.

Ensure that all staff are aware of the opportunity they have in every conversation with students to remind them of the possibility of staying longer or coming back. Without being pushy, or making a sales-pitch, it is professionally quite appropriate to point out to a student that their learning goals may be over-ambitious and that if they really wish to get into that university, or get that special job, then they will need to continue learning English to a higher level. Unrealistic expectations are arguably the greatest cause of language-learning failure, and we are doing our students no favours if we don't tell them.

Where academic staff are happy to advise a further course of study, if appropriate, you can make it easier by setting up a simple system by which they transfer a possible re-enrolment to your sales or reception staff for a specific quotation, without losing the personal contact. They should always follow up afterwards to find out if the re-enrolment took place.

As an incentive you can develop a 're-enrolment bonus' system where a proportion of all re-enrolment fees are allocated to a staff fund which is periodically shared among the staff involved, or among all staff on an equal basis.

You can as a matter of routine give all departing students a discount voucher which allows them (or, if you wish, someone else they choose to give it to) to claim a discount of a specified size on a particular course. This offer must be taken up within a particular period of, say, six months.

After students have left, it's worth keeping in touch with them for a certain period – perhaps a year, perhaps longer – with a personalized mailing, copies of your new brochure, dates and fees, and/or a simple newsletter. You may again wish to repeat the re-enrolment within a given period offer. Beyond the end of that period, ask them to complete and return a card if they wish to remain on your mailing list; and ask if they could recommend you to anyone else they think might be interested in receiving your information.

Agents' workshops

These are trade fairs with access restricted to schools and agents. They are typically put on by tourism organizations or associations of schools or government bodies concerned with promoting the industry as a whole, eg BTA for Britain or Austrade for Australia. The agents invited to attend are given a list of the schools participating, and they choose from this list who they want to meet. A schedule of these meetings is arranged, often with only fifteen to twenty minutes allowed for, in a large hall or exhibition area. This is very little time: for existing agents, it is enough to renew your personal relationship and to explain briefly any novelties you are introducing in the next year. For a new agent, there is just enough time to find out if you have enough in common to make a further meeting worthwhile. Such meetings can be arranged outside the workshop programme, or after the workshop has finished, for which reason it is often worthwhile arranging to stay on for a few days to follow up the initial contacts.

As it is a trade event, not usually open to the public, schools do not set up big stands. This distinguishes this kind of workshop from an exhibition: you do not need sophisticated audio-visual displays to attract passers-by. As you are selling to people in the trade, you will need all the relevant brochures and every possible kind of information sheet that might possibly be useful, not just about your school but also about local facilities in the town and region, travel arrangements, examinations, visa regulations, insurance and health care arrangements.

Exhibitions and fairs

These are aimed primarily at the public, although there may be special days designated for 'agents and travel trade', 'teachers' or 'business and commerce'. They are usually put on by commercial organizations who specialize in such events, and the tariffs for participating are high – a thousand pounds for a basic stand can easily be doubled by adding some furniture, a display cabinet, an attractive signboard, and a good-quality video system. As well as language schools, publishers are major exhibitors at such events, and suppliers of audio-visual and other educational equipment.

These exhibitions may have a programme of presentations attached, which helps to broaden the appeal of the event to particular sectors and to make it less nakedly commercial.

You clearly have to take a large stock of brochures, price lists, and any other 'giveaways' you plan to use. At busy times, you may have thirty to fifty enquiries an hour to deal with; at quiet times, anywhere from ten down to zero! Supposing on average you give out twenty brochures an hour to apparently serious enquirers. For an exhibition lasting four days of ten hours you would need eight hundred brochures. That's a lot of brochures, when you consider the cost of packing and shipping them as well as printing them in the first place. A smart-looking brochure with colour pictures can easily cost £1 a copy to produce. One way round this is to produce a flyer specially for the exhibition in the appropriate language. This can be targeted much more closely at the anticipated audience, and is therefore more likely to be retained and followed up by them. It is also a lot cheaper to produce; a single page monochrome or two-colour flyer can look as good or better than a full-colour brochure if it is designed well (avoid the attractions of do-it-yourself desk-top publishing unless you have some design experience available!). You can add a special offer unique to that event, such as a limited discount for quick booking, or a scholarship or prize draw.

Unless it is a small fair, it may be worth taking two people. A ten-hour day on a stand is exhausting; everybody has to take time off for lunch, to get a coffee, etc. A simple shift system that enables you to come in late or take half an hour off to wander round the other stands helps to keep you fresh (and sane). When a serious enquiry comes along, you want to be able to devote all your attention to it, and not to have to keep interrupting a client to answer questions from passers-by; but then, while you're dealing with one serious enquiry, how many others might you lose? An old agent or client, or a potential new one, may come to see you, and for a proper discussion of the mutual opportunities you need to find a quiet corner for a coffee or a meal. While you are so engaged, every time that someone passes by and pauses for a moment to look at your stand, you may be losing business that you've paid a lot of money to attract.

Exhibitions and fairs: procedure

- You need to attract people's attention.
- You need to distinguish your stand from your competitors'.
- You need to give them the information they want.
- Avoid giving them information they don't want or can't use, perhaps by stating on a poster the major types of course you do and don't offer, so that you don't waste their time asking, or your time answering, questions about services you don't offer.
- You need to give them an easy way to book or find out more.
- You can give them something to remember you by: a brochure or flyer, a business card or a small promotional gift.

Cost

Putting all the various expenses together, the total cost of participating in an exhibition can be considerable:

Basic stand hire	£1000
Furniture, lights, video hire	£700
Brochures, flyers, etc	£650
Freight	£100
Hotel and expenses (for 2)	£1000
Flights (for 2)	£500
Total	**£3950**

This is an example of the realistic cost of participating effectively in a regular commercial fair or exhibition for four to five days in a not-too-distant location. It does not include salaries.

Forward planning

If you are sending materials by freight in advance, find out from the organizers precise instructions for address and customs requirements (eg marking 'Printed papers – no commercial value' or whatever is recommended). Arrive well in advance of the set-up time and always allow a day, or at least half a day for the unforeseen. Breathe easily only when your stand is fully set up and fully equipped.

• •

True story   *Bonded brochures*

The decision to take part in the fair had been part of the long-term promotional plan, targeting the country where the big annual fair was to take place. The school's representative arrived two days before the fair opened. He spent the first day visiting a couple of agents and settling in. Early on the following day, he turned up at the exhibition centre in plenty of time to set up and then relax. The site was fine, the stand was ready and furnished exactly as requested. The only problem was, the brochures hadn't arrived.

The brochures had been sent by air freight ten days beforehand, but there was no sign of them at the exhibition centre, even after a thorough search of other people's stands. Several phone calls to the local agent of the freight company eventually revealed that, for whatever reason, Customs had impounded them, and the freight company had not been able to get them released. 'This sometimes happens,' they said. 'You must go to the airport yourself and collect them.' He did, immediately.

By lunchtime, he got to the airport (taxi: £20) and located the Customs office. Officials out to lunch. On their return, they agreed that the brochures were in their possession, and now that he had come to claim them, they would be quite happy to release them – from the bonded warehouse, about ten kilometres away. If he could fill the form in first. To do this, he had to inspect the goods in the presence of a Customs officer and sign to say that they were indeed his goods, were undamaged, and were for the purposes stated. Then he could come back to the Customs office to get the form stamped and the release of the goods approved.

He took a taxi to the warehouse (£8). The brochures were there, were in good order, and the form was completed. Another taxi (£8) back to the Customs office at the airport, form stamped and signed: 'You can collect your brochures first thing in the morning.' 'Tomorrow? Why not now?' 'The warehouse closes at four o'clock.' Back to the exhibition centre, to dress a large stand with a few brochures.

The next day was the opening day of the exhibition. He was at the Customs warehouse when it opened, got the brochures, took a taxi straight back to the exhibition (£22) and was finally on the stand by half past eleven, having missed not only the opening ceremony (no great loss) but also the ceremonial tour of the exhibition by the education minister and his entourage (annoying). Apparently, the minister had paused briefly to look at his stand.

MORAL: Allow extra time to set something up in an unfamiliar environment; always keep a supply of brochures with you personally; and take plenty of money for taxis!

Conferences and seminars

These are aimed at teachers and are often organized by teachers' associations. Their primary activity is educational presentations of various kinds. They are worth exhibiting at for:

- sales (if you are specifically targeting teachers as potential clients);
- promotion (if you are trying to establish your school in a particular country or region, and you want to get the name known);
- marketing (if you want to find out more about the system of English language education in that country, and how you can introduce or adapt courses to meet local needs).

Increasingly, agents and schools are organizing smaller one-day or half-day seminars to which teachers are invited and at which 'named' speakers are invited to make presentations on topical educational issues. The primary aim of the event is, however, to publicize the school or to sell the courses of the school or the agent. If well organized, these can be very successful sales opportunities which generate a lot of leads, and you might consider setting up such events yourself in conjunction with a local representative, agent or co-operating school. Invite a local specialist bookshop to participate (and contribute); give a scholarship, hold a draw, perhaps make it a social event. You can encourage members of your own staff to contribute to these events, promoting both your institution and their professional development.

Mailing

'Direct mail' means writing unsolicited letters to people, ie not in response to their enquiries. If properly done, it can be a cheap, effective and well-focused way of getting in touch with potential clients. If not well planned, it can be a massive waste of time, money, paper and postage.

Direct mail involves sending a more or less standard letter to a large number of recipients. 'Standard' and 'large number' because of the economies in time and work that can be achieved by automatic mail-merging (combining the letter automatically with an address list); 'more or less' because it is important that the letter is nonetheless personalized in some way, such as beginning with the individual's name ('Dear Dr Schmidt' rather than 'Dear Sir/Madam'), or 'topped and tailed' with a handwritten greeting, farewell and signature, and if at all possible a personalized message, however small.

A direct mail letter may be a regular mailing, for example annually to accompany a new brochure or price list. A more frequent mailing could take the form of a newsletter about recent events and developments at the school. Or it may be an occasional letter, with a variety of enclosures, such as:

- new promotional material, course descriptions, price list;
- a 'fill and return' card for further information;
- a discount voucher ('valid until ...' or for the low season);
- case histories of recent students or their testimonials;
- local tourist information;
- 'common questions and answers' to anticipate likely queries;
- a list of previous clients, especially in profession X or country/town/region Y.

A first-shot mailing is best kept simple because it's much cheaper to send, it forces you to be succinct, and therefore it's much more likely to be read: most people will glance through an unsolicited letter if it is a single sheet, but will throw a whole bundle away.

A first-shot mailing may be considered successful if it achieves a 5–10 per cent return rate. You need to decide in advance what you're going to send people as a follow-up at the next stage. If you've sent all your promotional materials out with the first letter, you've got nothing left to follow up with.

Where can you get the addresses from in the first place?

1 Buy them
You can buy address lists from companies specializing in them to meet your requirements by company, profession or region/country, eg 'major travel agencies in Venezuela' or 'pharmaceutical companies in Scandinavia.'

2 Build your own
You can build up a list of former students and clients, who unlike most direct mail recipients, have personal knowledge of the school.

3 From exhibitions, etc
You can compile a list of potential contacts from professional sources, such as lists of agents attending a workshop or teachers attending a conference. Most exhibitions and fairs keep a record of all visitors, and make available for a fee a breakdown by number, age, profession, company address, etc. Travel and tourist publications and newsletters are other sources of possible contacts.

4 From directories
National and international phone directories are increasingly easy to find, either in printed form which you have to purchase, or electronic form which you can pay for by access time – ie only as you use it. For example, the French 'Annuaire Electronique' has entirely replaced the old-style printed phone directory, and can be accessed (from outside France, with the right equipment) to give names and addresses by region of individuals of a certain profession or companies in a certain business or industry.

Visits and meetings

The sales opportunities described above may result directly in a sale. Frequently, however, such contacts lead only to an expression of interest on the client's part. This needs to be followed up by a visit either by the client to the school or by you to the client, during which, if all goes well, an agreement can be concluded.

Visits by the client to the school

Many clients, such as companies and agents, come regularly to visit schools, both established and prospective, to renew existing agreements and to set up new ones. They will want to see what changes have been made, for better or for worse; to confirm or refute the existing impressions they have of your school; to help them sell it by being able to give a more realistic description of the school to their clients and colleagues; and to see whether you have taken action on any of the comments they have made to you before! They will want to look over the premises and meet the administrative staff, particularly those with whom they will be dealing for enrolments. They will want to inspect residential accommodation or discuss the location and recruitment of host families in their area; they may well want to observe lessons in progress.

Visits by you to the client

Since an exhibition or workshop may lead to a large number of expressions of interest, you will need to grade them in order of estimated priority and value, long-term and short-term: visiting agents on their home ground is an expensive and time-consuming business.

An agent may invite you to make a presentation about your school to a meeting they have organized with sub-agents, teachers, interested parents or members of the public. Alternatively, a company may ask you to make a presentation to heads of other departments or to a particular selected audience of company personnel. You will want to be briefed carefully by them well in advance so you can prepare the most effective presentation, preferably in their language; if you cannot do that, and you have established that they will accept and are expecting a presentation in English, you will need to keep it simple, speak slowly and clearly, and use a lot of visual materials to reinforce what you are saying.

If you have already agreed in principle the terms of your co-operation, it is still worth arranging a meeting:

- You may want to explore the ground a bit more, to be able to show more responsiveness and flexibility to their particular needs.
- You may want to complete the agreement in detail: in most of the contact situations described above, there is not enough time or privacy to discuss co-operation in detail.
- Finally, it is a good idea to see more of the client and learn more about how they operate, and let them see more of you. Establishing a good personal relationship is a sound foundation to a successful business relationship.

4 How do you sell?

You have now considered what you're selling, to whom, and how to make contact. You've got a meeting with a potential new client, agent or potential student. How do you actually conduct the meeting?

Meeting the client

- If you feel time may be a problem, ask how much time they have.
- Find out exactly what they want.
- Tell them what you offer as standard, ie identify exactly the area of overlap and the areas of discrepancy.
- Negotiate on how to resolve the discrepancies:
  a what they want that you haven't got – an extra hour's tuition, a guarantee of no more than three of their students in one class, meeting at the airport, no charge for late cancellations;
  b what you're offering (and charging for) that they don't want – 'How much off the price if they don't stay for the last week?'
- If the discrepancies cannot be resolved on the spot, and you want more time to think, to consult, to re-calculate the cost, agree what further information or consultation is necessary, and agree on the time scale.
- Decide what action is needed next, who takes it, and when.
- If appropriate, summarize what has been agreed.

Price may come in at any point – probably they know your prices anyway, and would not be meeting you if the prices were wholly unacceptable.

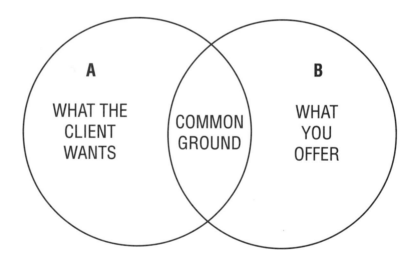

Fig. 3.4: The overlapping common ground is easily agreed. Co-operative negotiation is needed to resolve the areas of discrepancy: **A** (what they want that you haven't got), and **B** (what you're offering – and charging for as standard – that they don't want). This negotiation is co-operative: in other words, it is in the interests of both parties to extend the area of overlap sufficiently for agreement to be reached. Don't hesitate to say at any point that you need more time to think, to get more information, to check with a colleague that you can offer something.

If your first contact with a new client has suggested that co-operation is possible, or if a meeting has made substantial progress, write up your understanding in note form as soon as possible – immediately after, if you can. Then write to the client to seek confirmation that it is also their understanding. Even for an individual student, if what you have agreed or offered departs significantly from your usual programme, write a follow-up letter to confirm the offer and to keep a record for yourself and your colleagues to act on.

Summary

The thoughtful approach to a client is not to say 'This is what I'm selling – please buy it,' but to say 'What is it you would like to buy?' 'OK, this is what I've got, let's work together to see if what I've got can match what you want.'

It must be based on a genuine respect for and interest in the client as a person, not just as a customer. Everybody develops their own style of selling. Your sales style depends on your personality; the image of the school that you want to reflect; growth in confidence and experience; a desire to meet the client's wishes; and crucially, always being able to listen.

5 How do you enrol students?

The final stage of the sales process is making the enrolment. How well you do this will impress the client or the reverse, and will certainly influence their attitude towards your subsequent service. Particularly if they have only just made the decision to enrol with you, you want that decision to be endorsed as 'I am pleased that I have clearly made the right decision,' rather than 'Oh no, what have I let myself in for here!' Making the enrolment system work for the client as well as for you is using it to round off the sales process and to lead smoothly into the delivery of the services agreed.

Enrolment consists of three stages:

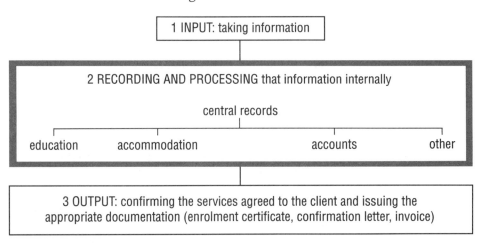

As far as the client is concerned, the middle stage is in a black box: she doesn't see anything happening, she can only judge by the input and the output. And she will judge!

Stage 1: Taking the information

How you conduct this depends on whether you make enrolments face-to-face or at a distance. In both cases, obviously, you can give the client a form to fill in. But if you have the advantage of a face-to-face meeting, you can make the process friendlier by having a member of your staff ask the questions (or at least some of them) and fill in or key in the answers. This engenders a feeling of personal service.

Stage 2: Recording and processing that information internally

This depends on whether you have a manual or a computerized enrolment system. The information has both to be recorded centrally and to be distributed to people who need it to complete the enrolment, eg accommodation section, class planning, accounts section. The 'central records' function is crucially the first priority for any incoming information or queries about bookings, because as soon as the information is distributed, there are multiple copies of it, and if some copies are updated and others aren't, then mistakes will follow like day follows night – promptly and inevitably!

If you have a computerized system which is accessed directly by the different departments, then the central records function ensures that the information is kept accurate and up-to-date. Since users in other sections will not know of updates, you may need a system of alerting people to significant changes such as new enrolments, cancellations, postponements, etc.

The most common manual system is a 'carbonless copy' form in triplicate or quadruplicate, whereby writing the vital information once on the top copy immediately produces identical copies for the other sections. Having the different leaves of the copy in different colours allows instant identification of which bit of paper belongs where. In a small administration department where perhaps only one or two people carry out the various functions, you can make do with a single circulated enrolment form, but such a system is more vulnerable to delay or loss of data.

You will then need a system to advise people of changes in bookings; a standard memo form or circulatory note is enough. To be absolutely sure that the information has reached the right people, you may want them to sign or tick the memo to indicate that they have read it and acted on it.

Stage 3: Confirming the services agreed to the client

This is not an afterthought but is crucial to the client's view of the transaction after it is complete, and therefore the degree of confidence with which she will look forward to the delivery of the services.

It usually takes the form of a single document summarizing the agreement that has been made, ie the services that will be rendered by the institution and the fees that will be paid for those services. Where the client and the students are different, there may be different forms of confirmation for each: and there will be a separate invoice or receipt for fees or deposit paid.

Chapter 4   Managing people

1   Motivating people

The key to successful personnel management is to motivate people to achieve the aims and objectives of the organization:

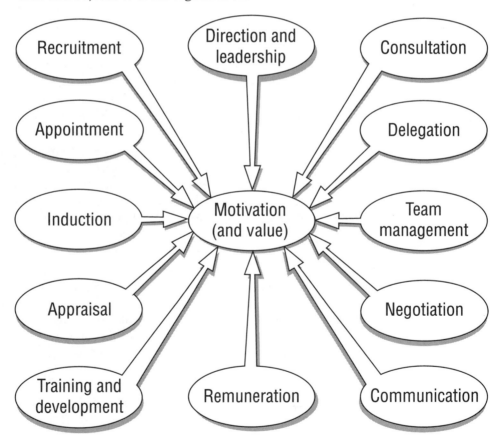

Fig. 4.1: How do you motivate people?

Motivating people is not a simple skill or a task you, as a manager, can decide to work on today, this week or even over a lengthy period of time. What you can do is bring about the conditions under which people are motivated, and you can achieve this by successfully applying a range of managerial and people skills in your personnel management.

The skills represented in the diagram on p 57 are by no means an exhaustive list and no one particular skill or its effective application is necessary, in itself, to achieving high levels of motivation. However the successful application of some or all of these skills may well be sufficient to achieve that aim.

Value

For employees to be motivated to achieve the very best performance they are capable of over a sustained period of time, they must feel there is a very real value attached to their work.

Very often teachers and other members of staff value each other in spite of managers rather than because of them. While this may result in reasonably high levels of performance within the classroom or the office, it is unlikely you will be able to capitalize on it, and it may well result in everyone pulling in different directions. This form of mutual value sharing is very important to any staff development programme and effective team-building but is no substitute for clear and unequivocal recognition of people's value by the organization, and by you as its formal representative.

If you have the means, you can focus on remuneration as an inducement or imposed form of 'contract' through which you expect high levels of performance at the expense of very low levels of people investment in non-financial ways. This is clearly very effective where the local conditions and working environment are unlikely to attract high calibre staff.

To effect change, bring about improvements and enable the organization to grow, you need a highly motivated staff. They must be clear that their loyalty, expertise, input and commitment are valued by you and the organization. It is not enough to apply managerial and people skills in a technically effective and highly professional manner: you have to care about people, value them, and their skills.

2   Recruiting

The mobility of teachers is, on the one hand, the reason that many people become EFL teachers and, on the other, a vital aspect of many language-teaching operations which may, by necessity, depend almost totally on short-term staff for the provision of their teaching services. Choosing and recruiting the best available temporary or short-term contract staff for periods varying from three weeks to nine months may then be a fundamental starting point in your management of personnel.

Conditions for recruitment may often be far from ideal:

- You may need people at very short notice.
- Potential applicants may be a great distance from you.

- Direct communication with them may be very difficult.
- Your needs may be quite specific.

How do you recruit short-term temporary staff?

You may need to consider some or all of the following when planning your recruitment process:

Recruitment process checklist

1 Analyze what your needs are.
2 Clarify the job specification and contractual conditions.
3 Provide clear briefing notes for applicants.
   Briefing notes should contain accurate, realistic and motivating information on the job, remuneration, terms and conditions, the organization, the country, locality, local conditions, accommodation and your expectations of the post holder.
4 Decide if and how to advertise.
5 Write a clear and motivating advertisement.
6 Design an application form.
   Application forms could ask for the following information: Full name, home address/telephone numbers, contact address/telephone numbers, nationality, sex, age, mother tongue, country of birth, dates available, educational qualifications, professional qualifications, career history, TEFL experience, name/address of current employer, present occupation and duties, languages spoken, hobbies and interests, health, relevant convictions, supporting information, referees, photo.
   Note: Check the local legal situation as you may not be permitted to ask for certain information in certain countries.
7 Clarify selection criteria and shortlisting/grading of applicants.
8 Decide how face-to-face interviews will be conducted.
9 Decide how telephone interviews will be conducted.
10 Clarify confirmation procedures for successful applicants.
11 Decide who will manage each aspect of the process.
12 Decide timing for each stage of the process.

Obviously your local situation will determine the importance, relevance and cost-effectiveness of each stage of the selection process. For example, you may well have to choose a successful applicant from the information on the application forms and references alone. In the case of temporary administrative or other staff you may need to add further stages such as a simple test of a required skill such as typing or word-processing. However the selection is made though, the preparation and planning of all the relevant stages of the selection process will help you to ensure you have the opportunity to choose the best available applicant.

How do you recruit permanent or senior members of staff?

While you may be willing, or may have to, apply a simplified selection process such as that outlined above for temporary and short-term staff either because of the cost factor, the urgency, or volume of staff required, you must do everything in your power to ensure you choose the very best available person when selecting a permanent or senior member of staff. In these cases the effect your choice will have on the long-term well-being of the school or organization, or some particular aspect of the operation, can more than outweigh any cost or time factor involved.

However well you prepare the selection process, there is no replacement for good judgement and very often this is largely a matter of intuition. Obviously some employers are better than others at assessing the potential and capabilities of people but we all tend to believe ourselves to be rather good judges of character in some general sense. The temptation to interview and select staff alone should diminish once you have seriously assessed your own capabilities as a recruiter and you can begin to look for the kind of support amongst your staff that will balance and complement your qualities.

How do you choose the selection and interviewing panel?

For some appointments two or three people are appropriate and sufficient as an interview and selection panel but for other positions a larger panel may be needed. The nature of the post radically affects the composition of the optimal panel for that position but the following factors usually have some bearing on the choice of your team:

- Do you have a member of staff whose judgements about staff and recruitment you particularly respect?
- Who will work most closely with the new member of staff?
- Who will the new member of staff report to?
- Is it appropriate or useful to have a staff/union representative on the panel?
- Do you have a member of staff who, as an disinterested party, could be useful as an impartial and objective voice?

How can the panel prepare for the selection process?

Essentially the stages of the selection process will be very similar to those outlined earlier. However, the panel will probably have to meet several times to arrive at an answer to the following questions:

Initial planning

- What are the job description and duties of the post?
- What qualities are sought in the successful candidate?
- Should the position be advertised internally, externally or both?
- What are the contractual terms and conditions of the post?
- What is the range of the remuneration package for the post?
- What will the form and content of the advertisement be?
- Who is responsible for writing and placing advertisements?
- What is the timing for application deadline, shortlisting, interviewing, selecting, and preferred start date?
- Who will respond to applicants and arrange interviews?
- Will applicants submit a curriculum vitae or an application form?

Planning the interviews

- What documentation are the panel to have prior to interviews?
- What are the criteria for shortlisting?
- Who will draw up the shortlist?
- How will interviews be conducted?
  - Who will chair the interview panel?
  - How can the various types of question areas be broken down?
  - Who will deal with each area and in what order?
  - How can the panel help to put candidates at ease?
  - Who will answer applicants' questions?
- Will there be a possibility of further interviews if required?

Planning the selection

- Should there be a uniform system or method of comparing the performance of applicants and their application, eg a grid to assess each applicant's merits with respect to the selection criteria?
- What are the selection criteria, eg qualifications, experience, personal qualities, interview performance, etc?
- Who is to make the ultimate selection decision?

Planning the appointment

- Who will inform interviewees of the panel's decision and how?
- What form of acceptance and confirmation will be required of the candidate within what time period?
- Who will follow up references and check qualifications?
- When and how will the appointment be announced?
- What information about the selection process should be made public to the staff, how and when?

Once the panel establishes an answer to these questions then it should return to the starting point and satisfy itself that the post is necessary and that opportunities to rationalize or rethink posts have been taken. Having planned all your procedures it may be difficult to consider that you have wasted your time but it is only once you have considered the details of the post offered that you can really assess the need for it.

Many of the questions to be answered by the panel are a matter of the practicalities of any particular recruitment and easily dealt with, but others, such as a job specification, require considerable thought since they are often used after appointment for appraisal interviews.

What is a job specification?

There are numerous ways of putting together a job specification but many would include most of these ideas in some form:

Job specification

Title of post   **Duration of post**

Reporting procedure
Whom to report to about what; when and how.

Aims
A simple statement of the ways in which the post is designed to contribute to the organization and its aims.

Responsibilities and duties
A general description of the activities, people and places the post holder is responsible for and a list of the duties.
One possible way of capturing the flexible nature of certain duties and the need for the post holder to focus on different areas at different times is to produce a tick-off menu of all the possible duties or areas of responsibility that may be required. This menu can then be discussed on a regular basis and the focus of the post adjusted and planned as required by ticking the appropriate duties for the period in question. A further refinement is to code the degree of involvement so that it is clear which duties the post holder has direct control and management of, which are dependent on the agreement of a higher authority and which offer a degree of involvement but no direct decision-taking power on the part of the post holder.
An alternative way of providing a picture of the post is to build a weekly or monthly diary of duties and responsibilities.

Targets
A set of realistic short- and long-term targets to be met by set times.

Review procedure
A simple but regular method of reviewing the duties of the post, checking targets and setting new targets with the post holder.

Planning your selection process carefully will help to ensure you make the right decision and are seen by the staff to be applying a clear recruitment policy, but it is no substitute for good judgement.

How do you manage internal candidates?

The selection process is relatively clear cut where all the applicants are external to the organization. You have the same amount of information about them and they all have a very equal chance to impress you with their ideas, approach and talents. The decision-making process becomes more complex when your applicants include one or more internal candidates. You know their strengths and weaknesses and you may well have shared in their experience and development over a period of time. The internal applicant may even have managed some aspects of the advertised post as a stop-gap measure. On the other hand you are also very used to thinking about their potential in certain ways and it may be difficult to envisage them in the setting of the new post.

Whether you decide to offer the post to an internal candidate or not, you will certainly have to consider their reaction and that of the rest of the staff to your decision otherwise the appointment could have a negative influence on the staffroom, a good member of staff or the post holder. This may involve an honest appraisal for an unsuccessful internal candidate and a very clear statement to the staff explaining the reasons for your decision. The involvement of a member of staff on the panel is one way to ensure that your recruitment policy is understood and seen to be unbiased by the rest of the staff.

● ●

True story   *Playing safe*

The new post was an important development for the school and much of the focus for the future depended on appointing the right person for the job. There was a shortlist of four but this was quickly reduced to two applicants. One of the candidates was internal and one was a known outsider who came highly recommended. The selection panel discussed the choice long and hard and eventually decided to interview both candidates again. The general opinion was that the internal candidate did not interview as well and probably could not take the department and role as far and as quickly as the external applicant. However the external candidate seemed stiff and rather cold in his approach. The panel decided to offer the post to the internal candidate because it considered the aims of the position would be achieved with less risk of 'upsetting the apple-cart'.

RESULT: Within six months the internal appointee resigned from the post because he was uncomfortable with the pressure. The external candidate had meanwhile joined a competitor in a similar position and was clearly achieving the very aims the panel had outlined to the applicants for the original post.

● ●

3 Appointing

Once you have selected the successful candidate and he or she has accepted the post then the contract should be put on a more formal basis. The legal and contractual side of employment is often very dependent on local conditions in different countries but, irrespective of these, there are issues which must be clarified at this stage. Where possible the following points should be clarified and included in the contract and terms and conditions.

Categories of information to be included and clarified in:

Contract	Terms and conditions
Formal statement of contract	Duties and responsibilities
Probation	Professional expectations
Salary	How and when salary is paid
Hours of work	Arrival/departure times
Term of employment	Punctuality
Employment start date	Dress
Additional hours of work	Rates for additional work
Confidentiality information clauses	Expenses
Holiday entitlement	Holiday policy, eg *when*
Sickness and absence	Procedure for absence
Maternity leave/pay	Work-related absence
Paternity leave/pay	Return to work procedure
Pension	Accommodation support
Redundancy	Other financial support
Termination of contract	Attendance at meetings
Misconduct	Appraisal
Procedure for dismissal	Grievance procedures

Teachers' contracts may be more specific and include policy statements on standby duties, lesson breaks, homework, lesson and course planning, observation of classes, out-of-school lessons and travel allowances, administrative duties, school property, smoking, in-service training, etc.

4 Inducting

Once the new member of staff has confirmed their acceptance of the post and signed their contract, the first few days or weeks in their post will be critical to the formation of that employee's attitudes, their initial performance and the speed with which they can contribute fully to the organization. The successful induction of a new member of staff depends on you providing the following:

- essential information;
- initial training;
- general support and a clear offer to help where necessary;
- some form of monitoring system.

What general information should you provide?

- copies of all publicity materials, dates and fees, etc;
- mission statement or statement of company aims and objectives;
- company structure chart (a chart which shows how the different companies or divisions of the organization are related and who directors and shareholders of each are);
- management structure chart (a chart which shows the main areas of responsibility for each member of the management team and who they and other staff report to);
- overview of who does what (a list of responsibility positions, names of post holders and their major areas of responsibility);
- staff list (names, qualifications, post titles, date of joining the company);
- information on meetings (a list of meetings held, who attends, when and where);
- information about in-service training (general information about the types of training available);
- information on accommodation, the locality, the country, etc;
- map of the locality;
- plan of the premises;
- fire/safety/medical/accident instructions;
- information on health and welfare arrangements;
- recruitment and staffing policies.

What specific information should you provide for teachers?

- teaching timetable (who teaches which classes, when and where);
- information on classes, levels and students (a list of students' names, nationalities, age, sex, returners, test/interview scores, agent source);
- information on resources and materials (a list of hardware, software, course materials. How to book usage of equipment; where everything is located; who is responsible for resources; operating instructions for hardware);
- course planning (information on syllabuses, coursebooks and supplementary materials for each level. How to plan a course and record lessons taught);
- course administration (information on testing, placement, attendance registers, progress testing, reports, dealing with student problems, etc).

Some of this information will be written, some verbal, some will have been sent as part of the briefing notes, some will simply be available for reference as required, and some of it should be presented as part of an induction meeting either with you or whoever is directly responsible for the member of staff. This latter meeting should also provide plenty of space for the new employee to ask any initial questions they may have.

What initial training can you provide?

In the case of inexperienced teachers, this could take the form of a reduced teaching timetable with a schedule of classroom observations and planning sessions with an experienced mentor teacher. With more experienced teachers you may need no more than a light schedule of classroom observations and discussions with senior members of staff and a regular planning discussion with the director of studies. Junior administrative staff would probably be attached to a more senior permanent administrator for hands-on training.

New senior members of staff would require time with you and other members of your management team to assimilate the feel of the organization and the necessary information on how it operates.

What general support can you provide?

This may be considerable in some countries where the organization is directly involved in securing accommodation, work permits and other legal documentation.

Otherwise it may be on the simple level of helping the new member of staff to settle in by taking an interest in them, finding out if they have any problems or queries and helping where appropriate. A simple but easily forgotten way of putting people at their ease is to show them round the school and introduce them properly to everyone in a relaxed fashion, ie not when everyone is managing a new intake.

How can you monitor their initial progress?

Although there may be a very clear system of appraisal and assessment in operation for all staff, there should be a more intensive procedure during a new employee's probationary period so that the organization and the member of staff are both clear about performance, future development and how they are fitting in with the aims and ethos of the school over this time. This will usually take the form of a series of planned meetings with the member of staff to discuss how they are settling in, to discuss their performance so far and resolve any difficulties they may be experiencing.

If the induction is half-hearted, rushed and ill-thought-out, you will run the risk of appearing unprofessional; the new member of staff will find it difficult to perform well initially and will become deservedly frustrated at not having the basic information they require to do their job and deal with the clients. If a new member of staff is successfully inducted into the organization, on the other hand, you will have optimized their initial contribution and hopefully demonstrated some very positive aspects of the school and the management which will set the scene for the future in terms of what you will expect and the kind of support you are able and willing to provide. The benefits of a successful induction will rapidly dissipate, however, if you do not regularly appraise members of staff and compare your and their perceptions of their performance with them.

True story *Chickens come home to roost very quickly*

Everyone was very busy with the new intake, people were testing, marking and placing students. The new teacher had been taken on at the weekend but was well experienced and the director of studies felt confident that with a quick chat the teacher could handle a short induction class with some of the new students. The class went well until some students from a particular group, who had been well prepared to think of questions to ask by their group leader, asked a series of useful and obvious questions about the course programme and locality. The teacher was completely at a loss but a returning student helped out with some useful and some misleading information.

RESULT: The class reported the misinformation and lack of knowledge on the part of the teacher to the group leader who phoned the agent at lunchtime. The agent phoned to complain just after lunch on day 1.

5 Appraising

Staff appraisal provides a formal opportunity for staff and management to reflect on and discuss individual performance, career development and any other relevant aspect of the employee's relationship with the organization. The result of such appraisals should be a plan of action which is implemented and monitored. How you appraise your staff will depend on your style of management but one effective way is to ask the member of staff to assess him- or herself as a starting point for your discussion. To facilitate a thoughtful response, some form of guideline will be required if it is only a simple form such as the one on p 68. This can be completed by the member of staff and also by the interviewer with respect to the person being appraised.

In this particular example the form is designed for a teacher. In the case of administrative staff you might ask them to comment in the first section on their accuracy, speed, attention to detail, planning, ability to deal with clients and suppliers, ability to work as part of a team, commitment and rate of work. For senior managers it may be more appropriate to design a tailor-made self-assessment form or use their job description as the basis for the discussion.

The self-assessment form, having been completed by the teacher and the interviewer, can then be copied so that each party to the appraisal has a picture of the issues each wishes to raise prior to the discussion. Alternatively you may feel it more appropriate not to show the teacher the form you have completed and may simply use it as the basis for the points you wish to raise in response to the teacher's self-assessment. In either case it is critical that you do not go into the appraisal discussion cold or having just read the teacher's self-assessment. You must complete the form in respect of the teacher being appraised and you must seriously consider how the teacher's perceptions differ from your own before you attempt to discuss the matter with him or her. Your aims with respect to that teacher's appraisal must be clear before the interview and you have to consider just how you are going to approach the discussion.

TEACHER SELF-ASSESSMENT FORM	NAME:

1 Under the following categories comment briefly on the areas you would like to focus on in the appraisal.

In-class strengths	In-class areas to work on

Out-of-class strengths	Out-of-class areas to work on

2 The second part of the interview will explore more specific questions relating to your performance and potential which may be raised by you or by the interviewer. What further questions would you like to raise? For example, which aspects of your work do you enjoy? What do you dislike doing?

3 What would you like to achieve in the next _____?

4 What is your agenda for bringing this about?

The appraisal interview should be conducted in an honest and frank way if it is to be really effective. The starting point can be a clear comparison of the teacher's self-assessment with that of the interviewer to discuss any difference in perceptions that may be obvious or become clear once each section is discussed. It may be the case that any such difference is irreconcilable and that you have to agree to differ on certain issues. You should not be afraid of this being the case and can often make this difference of opinion central to the action plan. You may feel it is appropriate for there to be two interviewers to appraise each member of staff as a useful way of demonstrating that you represent the organization's views rather than your own very personal feelings about the employee's performance. The disadvantage to this is, of course, that it becomes a two-to-one situation which may leave the member of staff feeling 'outgunned'.

The conclusion of the appraisal can be a form of contract between you and the member of staff, and there should be a written record of the appraisal, the action to be taken and the review process. This record could contain the information on p 69.

TEACHER APPRAISAL RECORD	NAME:
PERIOD OF EMPLOYMENT:	DATE OF LAST ASSESSMENT:
PERIOD OF ASSESSMENT: FROM	TO

Key points arising from interview

Further comments by member of staff

Action plan: What/how/by when/by whom
Criteria for achievement of action plan

Appraisal review dates:

Date of next appraisal:

Agreed by member of staff: Signature_____

Agreed by appraisal interviewer: Signature_____

This form can be completed by you at the end of the appraisal. It allows the teacher to record any serious differences between you both and provides the basis for an ongoing process up to the next full appraisal.

For appraisals to be successful the aims and process must be clear to everyone, the discussion must be completely open and honest and the action plan or contract must be followed up and monitored.

In summary, the process for this form of appraisal would look like this:

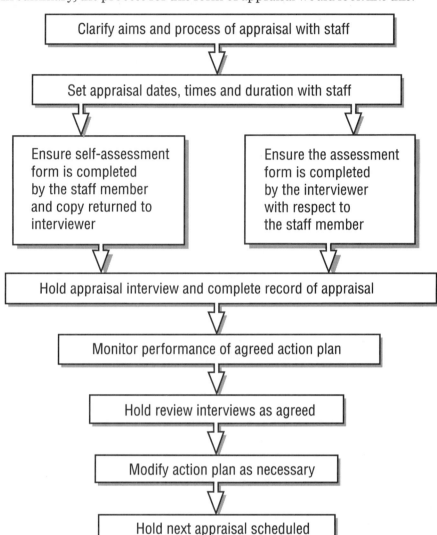

Fig. 4.2: The process of appraisal

This process of appraisal is only one form of assessment and will depend on many other more informal methods of assessment including classroom observation, peer assessment, discussions with the director of studies and involvement in the in-service training programme.

How do you deal with difficult members of staff?

Why might staff be considered difficult?

- their performance is inadequate;
- their performance is considered inadequate by clients;
- they are a disruptive influence;
- you dislike them, or they dislike you;

- other members of staff dislike them;
- you need someone more capable in their position;
- they do not fit into the company culture;
- they are unprofessional in some way;
- they have a personal problem which is affecting their work;
- they have been poorly treated by the organization;
- they have been poorly treated by another organization;
- you or other members of staff have mismanaged them.

There are many more reasons why you may consider a member of staff difficult. Whatever the reason you must first ensure you are clear about your reason or reasons and check the objectivity of your analysis against the views of colleagues. The views of other members of staff who are peers of the difficult member of staff may also be relevant. The simple rule is that if you are motivated by subjective or personal criteria in your assessment of them as difficult, you will almost certainly decide on the wrong course of action. To deal with a member of staff who is causing the organization real difficulties will require a calm, objective and caring approach. If they make you angry, frustrated or annoyed then analyze why and ask others to help you deal with them.

How can you deal with the member of staff?

- provide training;
- offer guidance and some form of external help;
- ensure a more sympathetic manager deals with them;
- move them to a less sensitive position;
- discuss the issue openly with them at an appraisal;
- issue a formal warning;
- rationalize and restructure the department;
- negotiate their resignation;
- given that you have good grounds, dismiss them.

You may be in your rights to use any or all of these strategies to deal with the member of staff but before you contemplate any serious action you must check your position in law, seek legal advice if necessary, and check you are following the procedures which should be clearly laid down in the contract of employment.

If you have made a real attempt to help the member of staff, have tried to understand the problem from their perspective, have used all the internal procedures for such matters and remain clear that there is nothing further you, other members of staff, external professionals or the organization can do to solve the situation, then you must pursue the more serious options however complex and daunting they may be.

Whatever the urgency and whatever the legal or contractual position, a simple rule is always to act and be seen to act in such a way that you are generous to the member of staff when compared with the regulations that apply. The reasons for this are threefold: firstly, any real analysis of the problem will probably demonstrate that the organization has not always handled the person as well as it might and therefore you have some culpability in relation to the situation. Secondly, if the matter does become a matter of law you will have been seen to have acted not only in accordance with the law but in accordance with the spirit of the law. Since employment law is never clear cut this will be an important factor for the court or tribunal. Lastly, your treatment of this member of staff will clearly show to you and all your staff exactly what your policy is towards staff. If you do everything possible to help the staff member and are clearly using serious sanctions as a last and regrettable resort, then whatever the opinions of the staff about the issue itself, your approach to people will be clear, will be noted and can only affect your staff relations in a positive manner.

Beware the danger of feeling the member of staff has cost the company a lot of money already and that therefore they are undeserving of any generosity or funds that are not considered strictly payable. If you go to law the costs, both in terms of finance and goodwill with other staff, will almost certainly be very much greater.

6   Training

Unless a very small organization you are unlikely to be directly involved in the actual planning and operation of in-service training. In most cases your involvement may be no more than deciding who is to co-ordinate in-service training, what the budget will be and ensuring that a coherent programme is forthcoming. Most training programmes include some or all of the following:

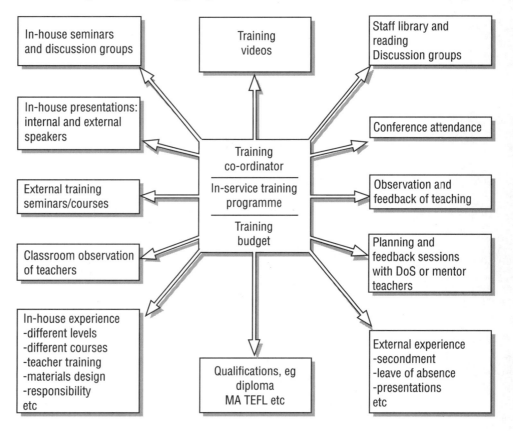

Fig. 4.3: In-service training programmes

It is very easy for all these and many other types of in-service training to be operating but in such a way that staff are unable to see or feel part of a coherent programme. Some form of document which pulls all the strands of in-service training together and offers a clear programme of events and action will help. This programme may also be directly tied in with appraisal action plans if it is to relate to and involve each individual on the staff. Very often the appraisal action plan can be a form of personalized in-service training programme which clearly relates to and draws upon all aspects of the general staff in-service training programme.

A number of types of in-service training may be dependent upon funds from a training budget but may also require some form of policy statement which has been agreed between you and the co-ordinator. For example, attendance at conferences, leave of absence, secondment, courses leading to further qualifications and external training courses all depend initially on there being funds available in the training budget, but they also require some form of policy stating who is eligible, who takes priority and how often these forms of training are available to individuals.

Administrative in-service training will usually include attendance on external courses to improve administrative skills and attain further qualifications, but a useful form of further training is to provide a programme of in-class observation and feedback sessions. This can provide your administrative staff, and particularly any registrations or telephone sales staff, with an essential understanding of the basic service you provide. Although it is much more difficult, teachers can also receive valuable insights into the administrative process either by shadowing administrative staff or by working for short periods in an administrative capacity. Ideally the programme for administrative and managerial in-service training would be incorporated into the one single staff training programme.

Staff development is an attempt to widen the professional development of staff beyond the concept of in-service training into a very much more personal model in which all aspects of a person and their interaction with the working environment are included. The organization can facilitate this process by providing the necessary investment, support and conditions under which people can develop their potential to the full.

7   Communicating

Listening and acting

The essential ingredient to any form of communication is the ability to listen. When any member of staff wants to talk to you then you should free the time required as soon as possible, listen to what they say and attempt to see the point from their perspective. Your aim should be to elicit as much information as possible and say as little as possible until you have a clear picture of what they are feeling and thinking.

Once you have a clear understanding of all the issues you should act as soon as possible. In many cases the best line of response is to set out a time schedule for further action which includes time for you to talk to others, consider the issues and find the right solution or course of action. It is important you agree a realistic time scale and stick to it. Once you have heard any other relevant points of view or sought the necessary information you require, then you should meet again with the member of staff and explain your decision. If the matter concerns other members of staff or changes then it is always helpful to consult a colleague or other manager about your proposed course of action.

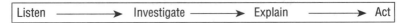

The point is simple and obvious. The skill can be difficult and may involve considerable pressure if the subject or point of view is controversial.

Interacting

Your personal interaction with people on a day-to-day or social basis is one way in which you can demonstrate the levels of value you place upon each person and the degree to which you care about them, their concerns and their future within the organization. For this interaction to be meaningful, the participants must not only approach their roles and functions within the organization in a highly professional manner, they also have to relate to each other as people. This can be deceptively difficult for it involves developing *yourself* as a manager rather than your role as a manager.

Essentially this entails building on your strengths and compensating for your weaknesses through the gradual acquisition of managerial expertise. The reality, of course, is that this process is very complex. You will learn a great deal about yourself and others while attempting to master basic managerial skills and formulate your general approach to management. You should always make the time to reflect on, evaluate and assimilate your own learning experience. This may help give you the confidence not to manage as if you were acting out a roleplay. In fact there is no reason why your development as a manager should not be just as much part of your interaction and discussion with others as their classroom and office experiences are with you.

As well as your interaction with members of staff you must also be aware of their interaction with each other. This may be very supportive and caring in some cases but you will also come across instances where certain members of staff clearly do not respect and value each other. Considerable facilitation may be necessary to ensure that the overall performance of those involved is not diverted to play a localized game of conflict at the expense of others and the organization. You may never succeed in bringing about good friends or even close colleagues, but members of staff will generally listen to your evaluation of each other's worth. If this does not solve the problem you should speak to those concerned individually and collectively and make it quite clear that their performance and that of the team is suffering.

Channels of communication

How do you plan a coherent schedule of meetings?

- What types of meeting are appropriate?
- Who might attend them?
- How often should you hold them?
- What is the purpose of them?

In some cases it may be possible to arrange and decide what meetings will take place for a nine- or twelve-month period at the beginning of the calendar or academic year. This immediately gets over the problem of spending a good percentage of time at each meeting attempting to arrange the next meeting, with everyone concerned studying their diaries and negotiating for their preferred date and time.

The schedule of meetings can be fixed as soon as major conferences, trade fairs and other relevant dates are known. Very often these dates are publicized well in advance and you can then take other factors into account such as public holidays, course start and finish dates, peak holiday times, very busy times of the year and any other events you can forecast with some accuracy.

If you get your schedule of meetings out early enough you can then insist that everyone puts the dates and times in their diaries and that they do not arrange trips, visits or any other form of absence on those dates. Obviously there will still be occasions when a member of staff misses a meeting for some unforeseen, urgent matter and you may even have to rearrange some meetings but on the whole, once it is clear that these dates and times are sacrosanct and that you expect 100 per cent attendance, then you have a reasonable chance that the vast majority of scheduled meetings will take place as arranged with full attendance.

You may wish to designate that most meetings take place on a particular day of the week so that staff get to know and expect that when meetings are scheduled they are always held on a Wednesday, for example. This can help you and staff with planning and reduce the degree of crisis management once you begin to get into the habit of checking your diary to see if meetings are taking place this Wednesday, if so, which are relevant to you, and consequently what action, documentation or ideas you may wish to focus on at those meetings.

A schedule of meetings for a particular period could contain the following information:

- type of meeting (eg General Management Meeting)
- day and date meeting (eg Wednesday 15 January)
- time of meeting (eg 14.00)
- duration of meeting (eg 90 minutes)
- location of meeting (eg Room 15)
- agenda compiled by (eg principal)
- action minutes taken by (eg registrations secretary)
- participants

Once you have the total list of meetings for the year, delete some 50 per cent and you may find you are left with a realistic target for meetings which will actually take place in the school. Your list will probably include general staff meetings, management meetings and administrative meetings. In the case of larger organizations each department may need to meet regularly.

Apart from regular staff meetings there should be a further channel of communication between you and the staff as a whole. This may take the form of union meetings or a staff association or council from which a representative is elected to meet with you direct. There are pros and cons to both. The former can tend to polarize the relation of staff to senior management and actually reduce your direct contact with staff. On the other hand, staff feel secure that the resources and experience of a union is a counterbalance to your privileged knowledge and the use you may make of it. A staff association or staff council may tend either to be so procedural and wrapped up in constitutional business that staff become bored and frustrated or so relaxed and informal that its purpose and powers are completely obscure. One advantage of a staff council, however, may be that it increases your direct contact with staff and theirs with you. In either case you should try to incorporate these types of meetings in the meetings schedule. The nature of this channel is largely unimportant but there must be some form of meeting, which is not simply information passing and chaired by you, where the staff can openly discuss and raise any matter pertaining to their employment and the organization with each other and you.

It must further be clear that you are obliged to listen, seen to be listening and clearly taking the views of the staff into account. If the school or organization is of any size, this channel of communication will need to be supported by some form of regular contact between you and an elected staff representative or committee of representatives, as any full meeting of staff is unlikely to be able to follow up issues, work out ways of implementing agreed action points and plan its own meetings.

You may also wish to encourage local teacher associations, directors of studies groups, union meetings and other activities of that sort to use the organization's facilities to hold their meetings.

How do you manage meetings effectively?

This will depend very much on the type of meeting but in the case of team meetings that are held regularly, there is a good case for providing an agenda checklist of items which are the concern of that particular meeting over a period of time, as well as asking members of that team to advise you of any matters or issues they particularly wish to focus on at the forthcoming meeting. You can then divide the meeting to deal with those agenda items which are familiar because they must continually be discussed and those which relate to particular projects, ideas or suggestions from the team. The management of the meeting may also be separated, with you chairing the first half where the decision-making process will be relatively clear and perhaps asking another member of staff to chair the latter half where the discussion may be more open, less structured and the decision-making process undecided. An agenda might look something like the one on p 77.

```
              Management meeting
    Date 15 May    Time 10.00    Duration 90 mins    Location Rm3
    Agenda checklist: 10.00-10.45              Led by:
    1. Financial                               Principal
    2. Marketing                               Sales manager
    3. Education                               Director of studies
    4. Personnel                               Principal
    5. Administration                          Principal
    6. Premises                                Principal
    The aim of the first half of the meeting is to exchange general
    information and make any necessary decisions using the above agenda
    as a checklist. Please ensure you have any relevant documentation
    if you are responsible for leading the discussion of particular
    items. The second half of the meeting will focus on the agenda
    below - please add any items you wish to be included and return to
    me by 10 May. The full agenda will be circulated by 12 May.

    Agenda: 10.45-11.30
    1. Finalization of dates and fees next year   Principal
    2. Marketing of new Christmas course          Sales manager
    3. Assistant director of studies post         Director of studies
    4.
    5.
    A.O.B items:
```

Some simple tips for running meetings

AIMS consider your aims and methods for each meeting	**DISCUSSION** check implementation of previous action minutes provide leadership without talking too much stick to the agenda ask others to chair the meeting where possible make sure everyone knows the aims of each discussion listen and ensure others are listening ask for opinions and ideas if they are not forthcoming ensure the mood is one of open and frank discussion don't allow the discussion to be side-tracked or hijacked
AGENDA ensure an agenda goes out prior to the meeting encourage teams and staff to add items to agendas	
DOCUMENTATION prepare carefully for meetings expect all documentation to be read prior to the meeting ensure action minutes are taken	
TIME start punctually keep meetings to a reasonable length of time finish on time	**DECISIONS** make it clear when and how decisions will be made postpone and call a special meeting for unresolved issues summarize action minutes at the end of the meeting circulate action minutes check action minutes have been actioned
PHYSICAL CONDITIONS ensure the physical layout of the room is conducive arrange refreshments if appropriate	

8   Negotiating

Basically most situations in which you will have to negotiate with colleagues are about the negotiation of change within the organization.

How do you negotiate change with your staff?

This change may be as basic as a change in the coffee arrangements for staff breaks or it could be syllabus changes, office moves, changes in administrative processes, new courses, changes in contract or terms and conditions, or the re-organization of whole departments. The option always exists, of course, for you to attempt to bring about change without any process of negotiation and the temptation is usually more appealing with very minor issues or major issues, where you believe the matter is too trivial to initiate a negotiation process or too important for the success of the organization not to happen. While the degree of time and necessary preparation may differ considerably in each case, your approach should be similar at least to the extent that you plan a clear process of negotiation, prepare fully, specify the parameters of the negotiation, listen to those you are negotiating with and allow enough time for the process.

The process of negotiation will differ depending on the issue addressed, how much involvement staff will have in the decision-making process, how many people or teams are involved, how controversial the issue is and the urgency of the situation. For example, you may decide as a result of discussions with your marketing team that you should offer a new type of course next year and advertise it in your brochure. You may feel that you must offer some form of course which fills the gap in your portfolio of services and meets a clear demand in the market. However, you may also be open to suggestions about the form and details of such a course and may be very aware that there are some serious implications, operationally and educationally, which must be addressed if the new course is to be a success. In this case, the negotiation process will need to be firstly with the rest of the management team and then with the relevant staff.

How do you negotiate a salary review with staff?

The particular difficulty with this one resides in the parameters of the negotiation. Who will make the decision and how the decision will be made tends to depend on the nature of the staff involved, the degree of job satisfaction they may or may not be experiencing, the current national political and economic situation and the financial situation of the company. Presuming job satisfaction is high, then as a general rule negotiations will revolve around the state of the economy and the perceived state of the organization. Consequently, it is important to ensure that the factual information you provide either to the union or staff council empowered to negotiate salaries, includes a very clear statement about the economy as well as the organization's finances. In the case of the former it is important not to have debates at the meetings about the rate of inflation, for example. Such information is usually readily available from government and independent sources and can easily be reproduced.

When it comes to providing management accounts for staff you are unlikely to have their trust if you show such figures once a year and attempt any form of massage in your interests. The benefits of sharing, discussing and providing open access to management accounts are considerable. Staff rapidly become aware that they are the same figures used in management discussions and Board meetings and begin to accept that you are showing the real figures whether they be good or bad. As in the example above, it is important for you to state what you believe the parameters to be. In a bad year you may as well tell people that you have little room for manoeuvre once you have taken into account the current situation of the economy and inflation. In a good year you should not be surprised to see staff negotiating for an above-inflation increase and you may as well publicly accept that this will be the case and that you will both be negotiating from very different standpoints with the expectation that both may or may not compromise.

Ultimately, you must be clear that if you wish to use experienced and committed people to their full potential then you must expect to negotiate a salary commensurate with your expectations of them and what the company can afford. If, on the other hand, you consider the annual salary review to be a battlefield where the only relevant factor is how you can materially affect the bottom line for the short-term future then you cannot expect the staff to respond well to any attempt to use their full potential.

However the issue may be more complicated than this, for permanent teachers may have very different expectations and concerns compared with temporary teachers or administrative staff.

Remuneration

An established organization will probably have a number of salary scales for different types of staff that have evolved over a number of years, with various modifications and additions. Undoubtedly any such salary structure is complex and very difficult to change radically given the salary demarcation levels that will be deeply embedded within it. Unless there are very good reasons for completely rethinking the salary structure and everyone is agreed that such change is necessary it is often wise to continue to tinker with the current system, however imperfect. Making wholesale changes to the salary structure can be very time-consuming, may involve subsequent changes to working terms and conditions and will not necessarily satisfy all or any of the staff.

Actual levels of remuneration vary considerably around the world and within many countries. There is very little comparative information on salaries available although some teacher salary surveys are produced by regional or national associations. In fact, of course, living conditions vary so much from one region to another that the only real comparison is with a similar type of organization in the same area.

● ●

True story   *A Merry Christmas to everyone*

The salary negotiations had begun in the middle of November. The company had performed reasonably well and had offered what was thought to be an acceptable increase to staff. The staff had responded and there had been a number of general meetings of all staff and meetings with staff representatives. The staff had made some alternative proposals and the implications of these ideas had been analyzed. There was actually little difference in monetary terms and everyone was confident they would come to some agreement well before Christmas so that the changes to salaries could be effected in January as usual. Then the staff representative was ill for a few days, some clients arrived for an unexpected marketing visit and stayed for several days, and before everyone knew it they were singing Christmas carols and saying goodbye to students for the Christmas holiday. Fortunately there was a general staff meeting on the last day and it was decided to use the opportunity to conclude the salary negotiations. The meeting started with everyone in good spirits but quickly deteriorated as it became clear that there was still a very minor difference between staff and management.

The issue had to be resolved and, given that everyone now wanted to be off to their families for the holiday, the principal made it clear the matter must be finalized then and there. The staff felt railroaded and although the matter was settled there and then, they left for the Christmas holiday angry and upset.

RESULT: The issue was no longer the details of the salary increase but the manner of the negotiation. It took nearly six months for the anger to die down and was remembered and referred to for several years to come when the time came around for salary negotiations.

● ●

9   Delegating

Delegating work and tasks is necessary for you and everyone else if the aims of the organization are to be achieved, and people are to be challenged and perform to their full potential. You will not be able to do everything yourself and members of staff will require you to delegate if they are to develop as individuals or as a team. Delegating is not allocating work as it arises or 'dumping' tasks you dislike performing or abdicating responsibility.

How do you delegate effectively?

Select the tasks
- What tasks have to be done by you?
- What tasks could others perform?
- What tasks would be a challenge for others?
- What would others do more effectively?
- What tasks will foster team building?

Select the person (or team)
- What time do others have?
- Who would be challenged?
- Who has the capability?
- Will their other duties need to be reduced?
- How will the team work together?

Induct
- What are the aims and targets?
- What is the deadline?
- What authority will they have?
- What time and resources will they need?
- How will they report on progress?
- What are the possible problem areas?

Plan and check
- Is the team or person committed?
- How will the task be performed?
- Is there enough time and resources?
- What further help and advice can you give?
- What problems are there?
- How are they being solved?

Monitor and evaluate
- How is the task progressing?
- Were the aims achieved?
- If not, why not?
- What was learned?
- How well did people perform?

Once you have delegated a task, you must provide the autonomy for the person or team to plan and perform the task with the minimum of interference from you. On the other hand they must be clear that they are accountable to you and must report to you regularly.

Why is it so difficult to delegate?

Many people find it very difficult to delegate. Their explanation for this usually contains one or more of these myths:

- It is quicker if I do it myself.
- It is me that will be blamed if it is not done well.
- It takes too long to explain how to do it.
- Who is there to do it?
- I need to know what is going on.

In fact, of course, the reason is often no more than a simple fear that somehow they will lose some area of responsibility or influence once the task is delegated to someone who does it well. One contributing factor to this fear is that you must relinquish the glory of success while retaining ultimate responsibility for any failure.

How can you help others to delegate?

- Review their duties, roles and functions.
- Guide them through the delegation process.
- Reassure them that their job and influence are not at stake.
- Discuss the development of their team.
- Demonstrate the process by delegating to them.
- Praise them for successfully delegating.
- Encourage them to delegate one task to one person as a starting point.

10 Managing teams

While there are many occasions when you may wish to treat the whole staff as a team you will undoubtedly find it necessary to build and work with a number of mini-teams with their own rationale, hierarchy and targets. For example, you may have several different teaching departments dealing with the different courses offered by the school. You will certainly have some form of administrative team which may itself be sub-divided into various departmental sub-teams. One of your major time-consuming activities will be to set up, build and manage a number of teams which may range from a team of teachers, senior teachers and director of studies to a small team made up of a cleaner and a caretaker.

How do you manage a team?

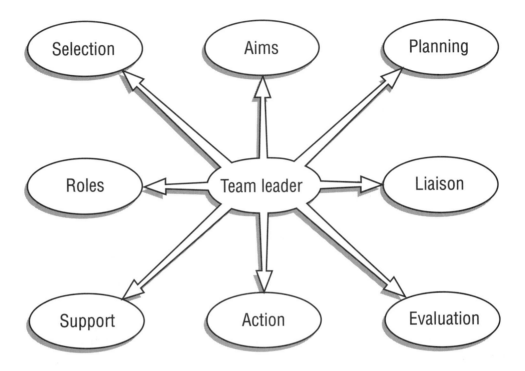

- You should select team members who complement each other's strengths and weaknesses, provide a balance of skills, experience and personalities and can work together.
- Clarify the aims and targets of the team to team members and other staff.
- Plan the work of the team and make sure everyone knows what they have to do and the time available to do it. Review progress and modify plans where necessary.
- Agree the channels of communication and ensure regular liaison takes place, information is passed and problems are known about and solved both within the team and between teams.
- Evaluate the cohesion and effectiveness of the team.
  - Do you encourage the team members to value each other?
  - Do you demonstrate that you value all the team members equally?
  - Is the workload of each team member equitable?
  - Do you encourage team members to support and help each other?
  - Do you keep everyone informed?
  - Do you encourage the team to spend time with each other?
- Monitor the activities of the team members, provide guidance and help where required.
- Provide the necessary resources and support.
- Clarify and delegate the role and tasks for each member of the team and make sure everyone knows each other's roles.

11 Leadership and consultation

There are many 'styles' of leadership and management. You will need to use all the following and many variations of them at different times, depending on the circumstances:

Imposing

For reasons beyond your control, the school experiences a severe drop in student numbers. You are very overstaffed and unable to continue the current level of staff costs. There is no indication that student numbers will improve in the foreseeable future. You decide to make one or more members of staff redundant and inform the staff of your decision.

Explaining

Your turnover is increasing but profitability is decreasing. You decide there must be a reduction in costs. You explain your decision to the staff and discuss the possible areas to reduce costs before finally deciding which to cut.

Persuading

You consider there is a very clear market for a Christmas course and try to persuade staff of the benefits of this type of course and the ways in which it could be staffed before attempting to make a decision on whether to offer such a course for the following year.

Suggesting

A change in the course structure causes a difficulty with the teaching timetable. You suggest a solution to the staff and ask for their views before making a decision.

Consulting

You consult with the staff on the form and content of a statement of aims and set of growth targets for the organization.

Empowering

Having made a reasonable profit for the year you decide to invest a set amount on improving the facilities, equipment and resources of the school. Given the financial parameters, you request the staff to decide what should be bought and how the money should be spent.

How do you decide which style of leadership to employ?

- Is an immediate decision required?
- How much time have you got before the decision has to be made?
- How important is the issue?
- Do you have a choice?
- How much knowledge is required and can be made available?
- How available are you and staff to meet?
- What are the interests and concerns of staff?
- Which do you feel most comfortable employing?
- How much do you need the agreement of staff?
- Are you planning far enough ahead to permit staff involvement?
- What style of management are you trying to foster?
- Are you willing to listen and modify your views?
- Are you willing to empower people to make the decision?
- Which is more suitable for the organization?

12 Concluding remarks

For you to achieve the highest levels of motivation amongst the people you work with, the answers to these questions must be clearly understood and believed:

- What are the aims and objectives of the organization?
- How can each person contribute to them?
- What style of leadership and management is preferred and why?
- Are empowering and consultation strategies available?
- If so under what circumstances will they be employed?

The proof will be 'in the pudding' of course: the decision-making processes you employ, the levels of remuneration you offer, the degree of consultation, delegation and effective communication you foster, and your expertise and approach to negotiating, recruiting, appointing, inducting, assessing and training of staff will all demonstrate just how much you value them and their skills.

Managing money

Introduction

Managing money is clearly crucial to the success of any ELT organization, yet few teachers, ELT managers, and would-be managers have any basic training in commercial accounting, or the evaluation of financial reports. They are often acutely aware of this fact, and are naturally hesitant when faced with financial management as a central focus of their duties. The concept and practice of double entry book-keeping is usually unfamiliar and the jargon of accountancy can be at least as inaccessible as that of ELT.

This chapter will not attempt to explain the former since you are unlikely to be involved in the actual processing of financial information, and will as far as possible limit the use of the latter. Certain key terms and phrases are introduced and used in the text but for the most part the aim will be to look at the management of money and accounts only in so far as it affects your decisions, planning and the management of the organization as a whole.

The two financial pillars of survival and growth for any ELT organization or company are **profitability** and **liquidity.** The management of money comes down to achieving a surplus of income over expenditure and ensuring an adequate supply of money to pay your bills and salaries.

Without a trading profit, or surplus of income over costs, you may well face difficulties with company directors, trustees or shareholders, but more importantly, serious losses will postpone investment in the future and will eventually result in a lack of money. Any long-term negative liquidity situation (lack of cash) can threaten the very survival of a company, however profitably it may be trading on paper.

Not surprisingly, your role in financial management is dominated by these two issues. Your evaluation of the financial situation, your decisions based upon the information and analysis available, and your management of cash may be critical to the survival of the company and will be instrumental in determining the levels of profit or loss at the end of the year.

1   Recording and analyzing financial information

Why is financial information recorded?

Larger schools or organizations may have a team of accountants, clerks and financial assistants to manage their financial affairs, but many ELT organizations are small companies or trusts and very often the functions of the accounts office are performed by an individual as part of their overall job description. The basic duties of such a department, whether it be one person or a large team of staff, are to keep an accurate record of all financial transactions and analyze them. There are several reasons for this:

- Governments require you to keep certain financial records.
- You need accurate information to assess the financial situation.
- You need to make informed decisions about expenditure and cash availability.
- You need to plan for the future.

How is financial information recorded?

There are many different ways of running the accounts of an organization depending on how large it is, whether it is fully or partially computerized, how many qualified staff are available and how much analysis of income and expenditure is necessary, desirable and practicable. Basic to any accounts system, though, is a record of monies received and monies paid out. This record is often referred to as the cash books or cash account.

RECEIPTS–	PAYMENTS–
all monies received	all monies paid out

Fig. 5.1: The cash books

Each transaction of monies in or monies out, in whatever form, is recorded or entered into the cash books as a receipt or payment. Receipts and payments may be in the form of cheques, cash, credit card payments or bank transfers.

As a minimum, the information you might record in the cash books would include the following:

- the date of the transaction;
- information concerning the form of payment or receipt, eg cheque number, credit card or bank transfer details;
- who has paid the money to you or to whom you have made a payment.

For example, you might record the payment of a cheque by the school to a travel agent for a flight or a credit card receipt from a client for services the school has provided. In most cases the transactions recorded in the cash books will reflect money moving in and out of your bank account.

In fact there are as many different ways of recording this type of information as there are accountants, but however they record transactions, the overall aim will be to analyze the income and costs in whatever way you and the accountant decide.

How is financial information analyzed?

In its simplest form, the accounts function could be managed by analyzing these entries of monies in and out within the cash books. However, most organizations would like a more detailed breakdown of their financial affairs than that immediately available from the cash books and would run separate books or ledgers to perform this analysis.

The main vehicle for analyzing financial information is the nominal ledger. It is, in essence, only an extended analysis of the receipts and payments recorded in the cash books.

The information from the cash books can be transferred to the nominal ledger and analyzed by coding each item to an income or expenditure code. The number of different codes you use will determine the level of analysis available to you and the degree of detail provided by the department.

For example, if a credit card receipt recorded in the cash books was in respect of sales from your school shop you may code the transaction to shop sales. If you want a more detailed analysis of your income from shop sales, you may sub-code the money received to book sales or stationery sales depending on what the goods were. Similarly you may wish to code staff salary payments to determine your teaching costs for each department.

The nominal ledger is often operated in conjunction with two other subsidiary ledgers, the sales ledger and the purchase ledger. The sales and purchase ledgers tend to deal more specifically with invoiced income and invoiced payments respectively.

Invoices to customers and any received income in respect of those invoices are coded or entered in the sales ledger. Invoices from suppliers and any payments you make to those suppliers are entered in the purchase ledger. For example, the cheque payment to the travel agent recorded in the cash books may be further recorded and coded in the purchase ledger. In this case, however, you will have already coded an invoice from the travel agent for the flight before you actually make the cheque payment in respect of it. If the costs of the flight were incurred as the result of a marketing and sales trip you may want to code the invoice and payment to general marketing. If you want a further breakdown of these costs you may decide to code them to a specific travel expenditure code within general marketing. In the same way you will want to code invoices raised by the school for courses to the receipt of monies for them as and when clients actually pay you. These transactions are recorded and analyzed in the sales ledger.

The subsidiary sales and purchase ledgers and all the information they contain are included in the main nominal ledger as well as all non-invoiced income and non-invoiced payments.

Whether you operate cash books or further analyze transactions with the use of one or more ledgers will depend on the degree of analysis you want and need. A very small school may quite adequately work with cash books by analyzing transactions in some simple manner as they are recorded. Larger schools or organizations with fully computerized accounts packages will probably have access to the full range and variety of analysis available from the ledgers and cash books.

As a further example you may wish to separate your year-round courses and premises from your summer course centre and treat them as two separate cost and income centres. You can now differentiate the cleaning costs for both buildings and operate a coding system whereby you post the cleaning invoices and payments made in respect of them to two different cleaning accounts in two separate cost centres.

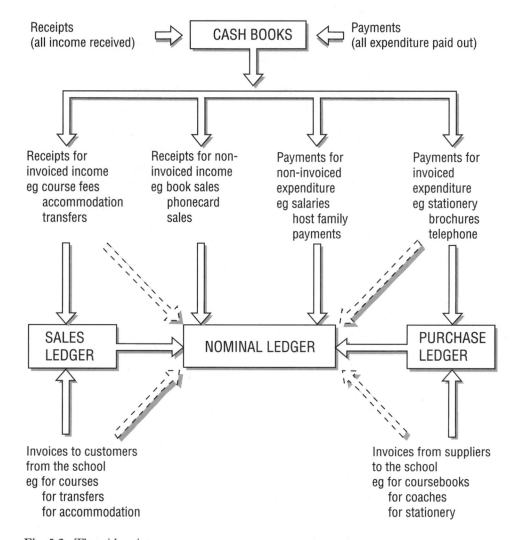

Fig. 5.2: The wider picture

What adjustments can be made to the accounts?

Your accountant will spend much of his or her time entering transactions in the ledgers and posting or coding these transactions to various accounts or codes within the ledgers. Once a month or on some regular basis they will close the ledgers and attempt to 'balance the books' for that accounting period. This is done by running a trial balance or statement of all the ledger accounts to check that they balance according to the principles of double entry book-keeping.

Computerization of the ledgers will permit you to access, analyze and produce reports and information relating to almost any combination of cost or income centres, codes and accounts within them. However some adjustments are necessary and desirable if the analyses you receive are to reflect the reality of the school's financial situation.

Transactions are recorded as they occur. For example, the cash books may record a receipt of monies from an agent for a course three months in the future, or a payment to a coach company for a visit to London some months ago. Similarly the ledgers will process invoices as they are raised whether they be for past, current or future courses. In order to ensure that the accounts and the transactions contained within them relate to the specific period of time you are interested in, the trial balance must be adjusted to ensure that only those transactions or invoices which relate to a particular accounting period are used.

The accounts must also be adjusted to reflect the current position of the company in respect of monies owed to it by clients and monies owed by it to suppliers. In the former case your debtors or the monies they owe are considered to be assets or part of the value of the company. On the other hand any monies the school owes to suppliers or creditors are considered to be liabilities of the company and decrease its value.

There are other ways that the analysis of the financial situation may be 'distorted' and there are a variety of adjustments which affect the value of the company and the analysis of how it is trading:

- **Accruals** – Your heating and lighting bills are likely to be invoiced after a period of supply. In order to present accounts that reflect all costs incurred by the business at a point in time, you will want to estimate or accrue such costs each month rather than as invoiced by the supplier. Other examples include telephone and fax bills.
- **Prepaid expenses** – You may find you have to pay for services and goods in advance of receiving them. You may want to postpone the inclusion of these costs until you receive the benefit of the service or goods. Examples include rent bills and publicity materials paid for in advance.
- **Deferred income** – You may receive income for courses to be taught in the future. You will want to defer or postpone the inclusion of this income until you incur the associated costs for providing the service. Examples include deposits for courses and course fees paid in advance.
- **Stock** – Your sales of books may entail carrying a considerable stock which you have to buy well in advance of selling. You will want to include only the income and costs for books you sell in an accounting period. The cost of books not sold in this period should be carried forward until they are sold in the future.
- **Bad debts provision** – A small minority of clients never pay. These costs must be included in the equation to prevent your income being overstated. You may have a general provision for bad debts you are unaware of as well as a specific provision for debts you know to be irrecoverable.
- **Depreciation** – When you buy a new language laboratory, you will expect it to last for several years. The costs of such items can be spread over a number of years by depreciating or diminishing their value over a reasonable period of time. Other examples include company cars and furniture and fittings.

The extent to which you adjust the accounts is often a matter of judgement based on the information available at the time, and while some adjustments will be applied by your accounts team as a matter of course, others may require a specific decision on your part.

Once the trial balance has been agreed and adjusted to produce an extended trial balance you can access the financial reports you need for a particular accounting period.

What information and analysis can the ledgers provide?

This table shows the information that can be provided and how this can be used.

Information and reports	How can you use them
Debtor analysis Who owes money to the school and how long they have owed it	**Debt collection** Chasing and collecting monies owed by clients
Customer account statements Breakdown of courses booked, commission receivable and debts owed by each client	Reconciling receipts of monies from clients Agreeing commission or discount owed to clients Agreeing debts with clients
Creditor analysis What the school owes to suppliers and how long it has been owed	**Managing cash** Deciding which bills to pay as cash is available
Creditor account statements Breakdown of goods or services bought by the school, levels of discount and monies owed to particular suppliers	Negotiating higher levels of discount with suppliers Agreeing monies owed Agreeing payment schedules/dates
Output tax report (eg VAT) Some countries require the collection of taxes on goods and services sold	**Collecting government tax** Recording the amount of tax to be paid to the government
Input tax report (eg VAT) Some countries permit the retrieval of some taxes paid for goods and services bought	**Claiming tax back** Recording the amount of tax that may be claimed back from the government
Management accounts – profit and loss Detailed analysis of income and costs Overall performance of the company Individual cost and income code reports	**Managing trading performance** Comparing performance with forecasts Decision-taking – managing expenditure – revising end-of-year forecasts – managing departments/centres, etc Preparing forecasts for next year
Financial accounts Balance sheet Statement of profit and loss	**Valuing and assessing a company** Valuing the company in terms of assets and liabilities Assessing current trading position

Fig. 5.3: Information provided by the ledgers

2   Preparing a budget

What is a budget?

You may have many plans for the immediate and longer term future of the organization, but if these are to be realistic and achievable they must be evaluated as part of an overall forecast of what will happen in the future. More immediately, you must attempt to produce a forecast for the next year of trading. To provide an overall picture for the following year you will need to answer the following questions:

- How much income can realistically be achieved next year?
- What are the costs likely to be to service this income?

A **budget** is a forecast of income and costs for the following year.

One starting point for such a forecast is the previous year's trading results or the analysis of income and expenditure for that period up and until you begin to work on a forecast. Using this as your benchmark you can begin to develop a budget by assessing any other relevant factors and their potential impact on the known figures for the last year.

Some factors to consider when producing a budget:

- income and expenditure figures from the previous years;
- course fee increases for the following year;
- salary increases for the following year;
- projected increases in general costs for the following year;
- changes in government taxes, etc;
- general EFL market trends and forces;
- trends for particular courses;
- general worldwide economic trends and factors;
- special one-off factors, eg contracts, riots, etc;
- changes in your marketing and sales policy;
- changes amongst the competition;
- projects to develop and improve the quality of your service.

Unfortunately the only concrete information you have is the previous year's trading figures and the results of your own decisions on fee increases, etc. Constructing a forecast or budget which takes into account all the above and any other relevant factors is largely a matter of intuition and informed estimation.

How do you produce a budget?

One way of producing a budget is to write a forecast for each area of income and expenditure for each month of the year, bearing in mind all the factors mentioned above.

For example, a relatively small UK organization may run a general English course for adults with twelve start dates a year as the core of its year-round activities. To produce a forecast for this course you can estimate the number of students and therefore the number of student weeks you can reasonably expect for each month of the following year. You can then derive a net income for the course for each month as in Fig. 5.5.

Budget for 12 months from ...... Income forecast for year-round general English courses				
Month	Forecast student weeks	Gross income @ £100	Average discount @ 11%	Forecast net income
Jan	120	12000.00	1320.00	10680.00
Feb	150	15000.00	1650.00	13350.00
Mar	170	17000.00	1870.00	15130.00
April	200	20000.00	2200.00	17800.00
May	160	16000.00	1760.00	14240.00
June	170	17000.00	1870.00	15130.00
July	230	23000.00	2530.00	20470.00
Aug	220	22000.00	2420.00	19580.00
Sept	180	18000.00	1980.00	16020.00
Oct	160	16000.00	1760.00	14240.00
Nov	160	16000.00	1760.00	14240.00
Dec	80	8000.00	880.00	7120.00
Total	**2000**	**200000.00**	**22000.00**	**178000.00**

Fig. 5.5: Income forecast

Commentary ■ ■ ■

For example, in January you estimate 30 students for 4 weeks = 120 student weeks
120 student weeks x £100 per week★ = £12000.00 gross income
Average agent discount for this course is 11% of gross fees = £1320.00
Gross fees of £12000.00 less £1320.00 = net fees of £10680.00
★The figures used are not intended to reflect current rates for courses in the UK and they are used for the sake of simplicity only.
Note: these figures take no account of any government taxes that may have to be collected. ■

You can apply very similar principles and produce a forecast for any revenue producing activity or cost area. For example, you may want to separate the costs of teaching salaries for each course as well as the income, as in Fig. 5.6 on p 94.

Month	Student weeks per month	Teaching hours per month	Standby hours per month	Holiday hours per month	Total hours per month	Salary costs @ £10.00 per hour	National Insurance tax @ 10.4%	Total salary costs
Jan	120	360	0	135	495	4950.00	514.80	5464.80
Feb	150	450	0	45	495	4950.00	514.80	5464.80
Mar	170	540	45	45	630	6300.00	655.20	6955.20
April	200	675	45	45	765	7650.00	795.60	8445.60
May	160	540	90	90	720	7200.00	748.80	7948.80
June	170	563	90	90	743	7430.00	772.72	8202.72
July	230	630	90	90	810	8100.00	842.40	8942.40
Aug	220	630	90	90	810	8100.00	842.40	8942.40
Sept	180	563	90	90	743	7430.00	772.72	8202.72
Oct	160	450	0	45	495	4950.00	514.80	5464.80
Nov	160	450	0	45	495	4950.00	514.80	5464.80
Dec	80	270	0	135	405	4050.00	421.20	4471.20
Total	**2000**	**6121**	**540**	**945**	**7606**	**76060.00**	**7910.24**	**83970.24**

Budget for 12 months from ……
Salaries forecast for year-round general English courses

Fig. 5.6: Forecast of teaching costs

Commentary ■ ■ ■

For example, in December you estimate between 20 and 30 students each week
for 3 weeks before Christmas
You estimate a total of 270 teaching hours to teach these students over 3 weeks
(eg 4 teachers per week x 22.5 hours per week x 3 weeks = 270 hours)
You estimate 0 hours teacher standby – director of studies to cover any absence
You estimate 6 paid holiday weeks at 22.5 hours per week = 135 holiday hours
270 hours + 135 paid holiday hours + 0 standby hours = total of 405 paid hours
405 hours x £10.00* per hour = £4050.00
£4050.00 x 10.4% Government National Insurance tax = £421.20
£4050.00 + £421.20 = £4471.20
*The figures used are not intended to reflect current rates for salaries or National
Insurance in the UK, they are used for the sake of simplicity only. ■

In the examples above you already have some interesting information to consider
which may cause you to re-think your forecasts. For example, the projected
income for the course over the year is £178000.00 as against an overall salary bill
of £83970.24. This gives a teaching to income ratio of 47 per cent. You may
consider this is too high or too low in comparison to other courses.

Once you have produced a detailed forecast for each area of income or cost you
can produce an overall budget summary and look at a provisional picture of the
year as a whole.

BUDGET SUMMARY	
NET INCOME	
General English courses	**178000.00**
Cambridge exam courses	**49920.00**
One-to-one courses	**6000.00**
Summer school courses	**95700.00**
Non-teaching income	**15750.00**
SUB-TOTAL	**345370.00**
TEACHING COSTS	
General English courses	**(83970.24)**
Cambridge exam courses	**(25459.20)**
One-to-one courses	**(3300.00)**
Summer course salaries	**(40194.40)**
SUB-TOTAL	**(152923.84)**
OTHER EXPENDITURE	
General costs	**(66475.00)**
Marketing costs	**(15500.00)**
Administrative salaries	**(61000.00)**
SUB-TOTAL	**(142975.00)**
TOTAL	**49471.16**
(Gross profit before tax)	

Notes on budget summary

An example of a budget summary for a small UK school.

Non-teaching income could include: book sales, bank interest, registration fees, phonecard sales, insurance sales, etc.

General costs and marketing – for a breakdown of what costs may be included see Section 3.

Administrative salaries could include all non-teaching salaries and possibly the salary of the director of studies.

Note the figures used do not represent current levels of income or costs in the UK, they are used for the sake of simplicity only. Negative figures are shown in brackets.

Fig. 5.7: Budget summary

Having produced a provisional budget summary, you can now go back and look at the detailed monthly projections for each sector and construct a monthly summary that can be used to compare your forecast with the actual monthly figures as they become available. (See Section 3.)

All the detailed mini-budgets involved in producing a summary serve two purposes. Firstly they are your forecast of how each sector or area of activity within the school will operate. As we shall see, this is crucial to producing a cash flow forecast and planning the future with confidence. Secondly, the budget, and each detailed section of it, represents a set of targets to be met by you and the team. These targets should be realistic and challenging. They can represent clear financial leadership on your part and should state coherent income and expenditure objectives for each department and team member. Although you should prepare the budget, you may wish to consult others about your forecasts and explain the assumptions and targets it contains to everyone. Rather than filing it away you can use it to define the financial targets and parameters of expenditure to members of the team and staff generally.

3 Management accounts

What are management accounts?

Management accounts analyze expenditure and income on a monthly or quarterly basis. When they are compared with the budget forecasts, you can see any variance between actual and forecast figures.

Once you have regular and accurate management accounts at your disposal, you have much of the information required to respond to changing financial situations in a fairly rapid manner, whether it be battening down the expenditure hatches, controlling and planning staffing levels or moving rapidly ahead with a development project based on an increase in income compared with budget. You have a clear means of apportioning costs, judging to what extent your budgets set at the beginning of the year are being met and how well the management team and departments are performing with respect to the relevant forecasts.

The accounts also provide you with real information which, if discussed with staff and staff representatives on a regular basis, may help the staff to understand how the company is performing, why decisions on expenditure and staffing are made and what the future may hold.

What are yearly financial reports?

Essentially much of the same financial information is used to produce both the management accounts and financial reports. Financial reports are generally public reports for shareholders and outsiders which provide information on a company's financial performance, position and value. Financial reports include an analysis of profit and loss, a balance sheet, in which assets and liabilities are used to value the company, and other statutory information for public consumption. Large companies may produce financial reports on a quarterly basis but smaller organizations would probably only produce a financial report at the end of the year. As such they are more applicable to owners, shareholders and potential buyers of the business rather than managers.

This chapter will not attempt to explain the format and content of financial reports.

What do management accounts look like?

This very much depends on what you want. It is your decision as to what is included and what degree of analysis is required. The degree of analysis you would like in your management accounts has to be weighed against the time and staff available and the sophistication of your computer software. However, you will certainly want to see a fairly detailed analysis of your general costs for the month and year to date. The report could look something like this:

General costs – March			Totals	Totals
Code		Costs	This period	Year to date
212	110	Pension scheme costs	200.00	600.00
213	110	Training costs	325.00	520.00
214	110	Recruitment expenses	75.00	90.00
215	110	Other staff costs	210.00	555.00
251	110	Books and materials	60.00	135.00
321	110	Bank charges	90.00	400.00
322	110	Interest on bank loan for lang lab	52.00	143.00
323	110	Depreciation	100.00	300.00
324	110	Bad debts	0.00	0.00
325	110	Credit card commission	50.00	175.00
326	110	Bank interest on overdraft	60.00	320.00
331	110	Rent	800.00	2400.00
332	110	Rates	400.00	1200.00
333	110	Light and heat	500.00	1500.00
334	110	Cleaning costs	300.00	900.00
335	110	Repairs and renewals	950.00	1250.00
336	110	Insurances	100.00	300.00
351	110	Legal and professional costs	35.00	35.00
352	110	Subscriptions	22.00	66.00
361	110	Telephone, telex and fax	485.00	1455.00
362	110	Postage and courier	800.00	2200.00
371	110	Staff travel and subsistence	365.00	1060.00
381	110	Equipment – minor purchases	45.00	120.00
382	110	Equipment – maintenance	88.00	264.00
383	110	Equipment – hire and lease	120.00	360.00
384	110	Photocopier costs	300.00	800.00
391	110	Printing and stationery	100.00	200.00
392	110	Office and general costs	55.00	145.00
		Total	6687.00	17493.00
		Budget forecast	5540.00	16620.00

Note: These figures are not intended to show the actual level of costs an organization might incur, the columns are completed for the sake of the example only. 110 is the main code for general costs.

Fig. 5.8: Management accounts – analysis of costs

In the example on p 97 general costs are clearly greater than your budget forecast. This may be understandable and acceptable if income is also greater than forecast. If the latter is not the case you may conclude your budget for general costs is unrealistic, change your budget or decide to reduce your expenditure over the next few months. It may not be that easy to reduce general costs since a large proportion of them are fixed or unchangeable, eg rent. There are some costs, however, such as repairs and renewals, that you can affect immediately once you decide to act. The summary of your management accounts will provide you with a bottom line for the month and the year to date:

Management accounts – March				
NET INCOME	**March actual**	**March budget**	**Year to date actual**	**Year to date budget**
General English courses	13552.65	15130.00	33102.45	39160.00
Cambridge exam courses	1580.00	2080.00	1580.00	2080.00
One-to-one courses	450.00	500.00	1300.00	1400.00
Summer school courses	0.00	0.00	0.00	0.00
Non-teaching income	1100.00	1200.00	3480.00	3640.00
SUB-TOTAL	**16682.65**	**18910.00**	**39462.45**	**46280.00**
TEACHING COSTS				
General English courses	(6800.00)	(6955.20)	(17540.00)	(17884.80)
Cambridge exam courses	(800.00)	(1000.00)	(800.00)	(1000.00)
One-to-one courses	(250.00)	(270.00)	(650.00)	(750.000)
Summer courses	0.00	0.00	0.00	0.00
SUB-TOTAL	**(7850.00)**	**(8225.20)**	**(18990.00)**	**(19634.80)**
OTHER EXPENDITURE				
General costs	(6687.00)	(6000.00)	(17493.00)	(18000.00)
Marketing costs	(1300.00)	(1200.00)	(3800.00)	(3600.00)
Administrative salaries	(4400.00)	(4500.00)	(13300.00)	(13500.00)
SUB-TOTAL	**(12387.00)**	**(11700.00)**	**(34593.00)**	**(35100.00)**
Profit/loss before tax	**(3554.35)**	**(1015.20)**	**(14120.55)**	**(8454.80)**

Fig. 5.9: Management accounts – summary

Commentary ■ ■ ■

If you look back to the budget in Section 2 (p 93) you can see how the salaries and income for general English courses both for March and the three months cumulatively relate directly to the figures given in the above budget columns. Similarly you can see an indirect relationship between the budget summary and the above forecast figures for other sectors. For example, the total budget for general costs was 66475.00. If you divide this figure by twelve for an average monthly cost, you can see that the forecast figure for March and the first three months of the year is higher than the average. The decision to budget a slightly higher figure than average for these months may be the result of past experience or because you intend to spend much of your repairs and renewals budget early in the year. Note that negative figures are shown in brackets here. ■

You may wish to summarize further all your actual monthly and year to date results alongside your forecasts for each period in order that you can see any trends that may emerge and the variance between actual and forecast figures at a glance.

For the purposes of looking at this complete form of summary, the example used is of a slightly larger organization – see pp 100 and 101.

Explanatory notes – Overall summary of management accounts (pp 100 and 101)

This organization manages its accounts on the basis of thirteen periods per year, each of which is four weeks in length. Negative figures are shown with a minus sign here.

The gross profit or loss total is simply the net income for the period, less all expenditure before corporation tax.

You can use the accounts to compare the actual results with the forecast for the first three periods. For example, in period 2 the school was budgeted to lose £10500 but in fact only lost £9850. The variance figure shows the difference to be a positive one to the extent of £650. The accumulated variance figure shows the variance between budget and actual over the two combined periods.

The P1–13 budget column, towards the end of the accounts, shows you the budget for the entire year. The P1–13 forecast column shows a combined figure based on the actual results for P1 to P3 added to the budgeted forecast for the other ten periods. In effect this comparison provides a revised forecast for end of year profits based on the variance between actual and forecast so far. In this particular case the variance figure for the first three periods shows an accumulated improvement on budget of £1150 and this is mirrored in the revised forecast for end of year profits of £71150 rather than the £70000 budgeted in the forecast column.

The final two columns on the accounts show the cumulative position year to date, ie the combined budget for periods 1 to 3 compared with the actual for those periods. Again it shows the school is losing less than budgeted to the tune of £1150.

Management Accounts – Monthly Summary

Summary	P1 Budget	P1 Actual	P2 Budget	P2 Actual	P3 Budget	P3 Actual	P4 Budget	P4 Actual	P5 Budget	P5 Actual	P6 Budget	P6 Actual	P7 Budget	P7 Actual	P8 Budget
Income															
Term Income	20000	18900	35000	36000	35000	36500	36000		37000		37000		45000		45000
One-to-One-Income	3000	2600	5000	5400	6000	7200	7000		6000		9000		12000		15000
Cambridge Income	0	0	0	0	12500	12000	25000		25000		12500		0		0
Summer Holiday School Income	0	0	0	0	0	0	0		0		0		61000		125000
Sub Total	23000	21500	40000	41400	53500	55700	68000		68000		58500		118000		185000
Additional Income	1000	1500	1500	1550	1500	1650	2000		2500		3000		3500		6000
Total Income	24000	23000	41500	42950	55000	57350	70000		70500		61500		121500		191000
Salaries															
*Term Salaries	–14000	–13500	–16000	–16500	–16000	–17000	–16000		–16000		–16000		–18000		–20000
One-to-One-Salaries	–1500	–1400	–2500	–2800	–3000	–3700	–3500		–3500		–4500		–7000		–7000
Cambridge Salaries					–6000	–6000	–11500		–11500		–6000				
Summer Holiday School Salaries													–30000		–40000
Total Salaries	–15500	–14900	–18500	–19300	–25000	–26700	–31000		–31000		–26500		–55000		–67000
Expenditure															
Admin Salaries	–14500	–14350	–14500	–14600	–14500	–14450	–14500		–14500		–15500		–16500		–20000
Marketing Costs	–4000	–3800	–4000	–4100	–5000	–4300	–5000		–5000		–6000		–6000		–6000
General Costs	–13000	–13750	–15000	–14800	–15000	–15100	–15000		–15000		–17000		–20000		–25000
Total Costs	–31500	–31900	–33500	–33500	–34500	–33850	–34500		–34500		–38500		–42500		–51000
Gross P/L	**–23000**	**–23800**	**–10500**	**–9850**	**–4500**	**–3200**	**4500**	**0**	**5000**	**0**	**–3500**	**0**	**24000**	**0**	**73000**
Variance		–800		650		1300									
Variance Acc.		–800		–150		1150									

Actual for period 1 to 3

Management Accounts – Monthly Summary

Summary	P8	P9	P9	P10	P10	P11	P11	P12	P12	P13	P13	P1–13	P1–13	P1–3	P1–3
	Actual	Budget	Actual	Budget	Actual	Budget	Actual	Budget	Actual	Budget	Actual	Budget	Forecast	Acc Bud	Acc Act
Income															
Term Income		40000		37000		37000		37000		24000		465000	466400	90000	91400
One-to-One-Income		10000		8000		8000		7000		4000		100000	101200	14000	15200
Cambridge Income		0		12500		25000		25000		12500		150000	149500	12500	12000
Summer Holiday School Income		64000		0		0		0		0		250000	250000	0	0
Sub Total		114000		57500		70000		69000		40500		965000	967100	116500	118600
Additional Income		5000		3000		2500		2000		1500		35000	35700	4000	4700
Total Income		119000		60500		72500		71000		42000		1000000	1002800	120500	123300
Salaries															
Term Salaries		-18000		-16000		-16000		-15000		-13000		-210000	-211000	-46000	-47000
One-to-One-Salaries		-4500		-4000		-4000		-3000		-2000		-50000	-50900	-7000	-7900
Cambridge Salaries				-6000		-11500		-11500		-6000		-70000	-70000	-6000	-6000
Summer Holiday School Salaries		-30000										-100000	-100000	0	0
Total Salaries		-52500		-26000		-31500		-29500		-21000		-430000	-431900	-59000	-60900
Expenditure															
Admin. Salaries		-20000		-17000		-14500		-14500		-14500		-205000	-204900	-43500	-43400
Marketing Costs		-5000		-6000		-7500		-7500		-3000		-70000	-69200	-13000	-12200
General Costs		-25000		-17000		-15000		-15000		-18000		-225000	-225650	-43000	-43650
Total Costs		-50000		-40000		-37000		-37000		-35500		-500000	-499750	-99500	-99250
Gross P/L	0	16500	0	-5500	0	4000	0	4500	0	-14500	0	70000	71150	-38000	-36850
Variance	0	0	0	0	0	0	0	0	0	0	0	0	0	0	0
Variance Acc	0	0	0	0	0	0	0	0	0	0	0	0	0	0	1150

Actual for period 1 to 3

4 Managing cash flow

Cash flow is the movement of money in and out of the organization. If you always have more coming in than going out you will not have a problem. Unfortunately this is seldom the case for any company. The management accounts in the preceding section may show that you expect to trade at a loss for the first three accounting periods of the year but this does not imply that you will necessarily have a cash problem. You may receive deposits or payments in advance for your summer business, or you may have made considerable profits in the preceding year which can be used as a cushion through the winter. Similarly you may be confident of achieving a surplus of income over expenditure by the end of the year but this will not help you, if after a busy summer, you are owed so much money that you experience difficulty in paying your bills. In fact of course you will look carefully at your projected cash flow at any time when you know you will be trading at a loss, and your chances of weathering a severe cash flow crisis are certainly going to be improved if you are clearly making profits at the end of the year.

How do you plan your cash flow?

In the same way that a budget was required for measuring success in terms of profitability, a forecast is required for cash flow. The cash flow forecast is based upon the budget in terms of expected fees and costs but your cash flow forecast must also take into account all those factors that were intentionally removed from the budget equation. These include costs that play no part in the assessment of profitability because you are collecting the money for others, eg government taxes, accommodation costs, commission, etc.

When it comes to estimating cash flow, however, these payments and other large movements of cash which may have been adjusted in the period management accounts but have to be paid in full at the time of delivery must be taken into account when estimating how much cash will move into and out of your bank account each week and month.

In the case of invoiced income and expenditure the management accounts may be showing considerable income for March but all this means is that you have raised invoices to that amount, not that you have actually been paid any of those fees in that month. In terms of cash flow you may not expect to receive that income until May or much later.

As in the case of the budget, the actual cash flow graph for the previous year is an important source of information when you are producing a cash flow forecast but obviously the changing calendar and any known factors such as price increases, wage increases, new business, lost business, etc which might cause differences in cash flow must be taken into consideration.

What does a cash flow analysis look like?

The example below summarizes a cash flow analysis for a year. This organization also manages its accounts on the basis of thirteen periods per year, each of which is four weeks in length (P1–P13). Negative figures are shown with a minus sign.

The cash flow is stated in thousands and is actual for the first three periods and a forecast for periods 4–13.

The **opening balance** is the amount of cash in the bank at the beginning of the period. This figure is the same as the closing balance of the previous period.
Receipts include any monies received in the period – you may wish to analyze sales ledger receipts and other types of monies received, eg book sales, excursion income, etc.
Payments include any monies paid out and may also be analyzed into various categories including purchase ledger payments, VAT, accommodation, salaries, etc.
The **closing balance** is the amount of cash left in the bank at the end of the period and is the same as the opening balance of the next period.
The **period movement** is simply the difference between receipts and payments or monies in and out.
The **YTD movement**, or accumulated year to date movement, is the accumulated difference from the start of the year – how much you gain or lose in real terms.
The **bank balance** shows the actual bank situation at the close of each period and differs from the closing cash balance because there are always cheques for payments which are in the cash flow but have not at that time been presented at the bank.

In the case of cash flow, the need to revise your forecast once actual results are available is critical, since any shortfall on forecast will cause problems later which may require assistance. The actual results for P1–3 are fed into the cash flow forecast and the forecast for the remaining periods is revised accordingly.

Cash Flow Summary – actual for P1–3 (1000's)													
Period	1	2	3	4	5	6	7	8	9	10	11	12	13	Latest
Act or F'cast	Act	Act	Act	F'cast	F'cast	F'cast	F'cast	F'cast	F'cast	F'cast	F'cast	F'cast	F'cast	Forecast
Opening balance	30	20	0	−10	−60	−45	10	50	150	60	50	30	45	30
Receipts	120	125	110	90	140	200	400	600	300	375	240	225	250	3175
Payments	130	145	120	140	125	145	360	500	390	385	260	210	240	3150
Closing balance	20	0	−10	−60	−45	10	50	150	60	50	30	45	55	55
Period movement	−10	−20	−10	−50	15	55	40	100	−90	−10	−20	15	10	
YTD movement	−10	−30	−40	−90	−75	−20	20	120	30	20	0	15	25	
Bank Balance	25	6	−5											

Fig. 5.10: Cash flow analysis

How do you monitor cash flow?

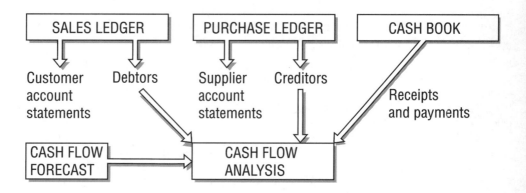

Obtaining the actual information for you to control cash flow each week and each period entails monitoring and evaluating a range of factors. You have to be informed or aware of the level of receipts, both in terms of what comes directly into the organization and in terms of monies received by the bank on behalf of the organization. Similarly, you have to control your payments to creditors. You must monitor the variance between your projected levels of income and expenditure as estimated in the cash flow forecast and the actual results as they become known. In short, you must be clear about how much you spend, how much you owe, how much you receive and what you are owed.

The cash flow forecast for the year is based upon weekly forecasts which may give a very detailed breakdown of the various types of receipts and payments expected in that week.

You will know when an overdraft facility is required and when monies are available to be moved to the deposit account to gain interest. More importantly though, as the actual results are fed into the cash flow analysis, you can monitor very closely any shortfall of receipts and approaching liquidity problems before the need for short-term funds becomes unmanageable and it is too late for action.

How can you improve cash flow?

- The quickest way to improve cash flow is to chase debtors and get the money in as fast as possible.
- As a very short-term move, you can withhold payments due to creditors, but if you fall too far behind with payments you will find creditors taking action to recover their debts.
- You can control or cut expenditure and reduce payments going out over a period of time.
- You can try to induce larger agents to pay some money in advance as part of an agreed payment schedule.
- You can try to increase general levels of income through greater sales of courses and other services.
- You can dispose of assets and free the cash from the sale for trading.

- You can go to the bank and arrange an overdraft facility or loan. The bank will usually accommodate you under the following conditions:
  - you demonstrate you are in control of the situation, your forecasts are realistic and your accounts are up-to-date;
  - the need is clearly short term and you have planned for it;
  - you are trading profitably over a period of time;
  - you have some form of collateral to offer as security;
  - the company is fundamentally sound.

5 Your role in managing money

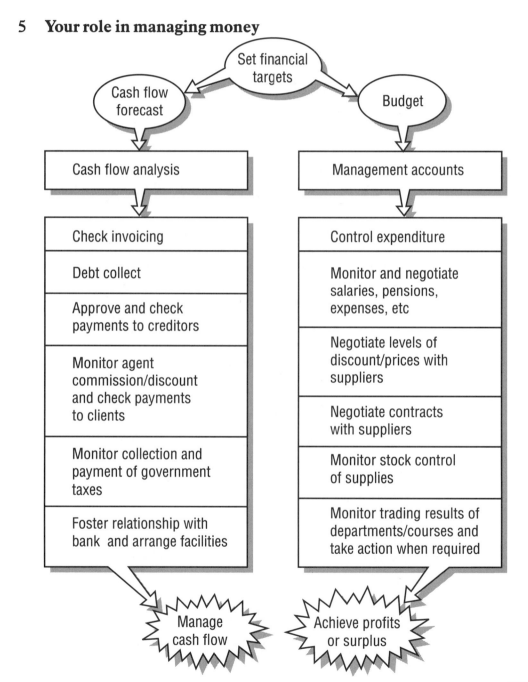

Chapter 6 Managing continuing operations

Introduction

This chapter is concerned with aspects of continuing operations (usually all year round), in contrast with Chapter 7, which looks at short courses.

In the management of continuing operations, one of the most difficult tasks is to 'stay fresh'. While you and your staff can judge how things are going over the long term, and know that a not-so-good course is balanced by several sound ones, students will make up their minds on their first course. You have to be able not only to treat each student as an individual, but to re-invent the best course and the most personal attention each time, for every student.

1 How is the school presented to students?

It is both important and difficult to look at your school or programme from a student's point of view. How do *they* see it? In particular, what are their first impressions? Again and again, feedback from sponsors and agents as well as from students concerns the packaging or presentation of the programme: not the obvious central features, such as teaching or homestay, but intangible things like *treating each person as an individual*, not just another student (administrative and management staff as well as teachers must learn and use names!). The first-day procedure is also crucial:

First-day procedure

Show a genuine personal welcome to and interest in newcomers (offering a safe haven and mediation with a strange environment).

Carry out fast, efficient and accurate placement testing, so that the time-conscious don't feel that teaching time is being wasted.

Provide the basic information, a clear and concise introduction to school procedures and to the local environment.

Identify key staff and other sources of further information.

Anticipate likely questions and problems (post office, changing money, bank account, contact family, re-confirm tickets, etc).

Take an immediate first step in the social programme.

Ensure host families are aware of the first-day procedure and can help put students at ease.

As a brainstorming exercise, you might like to sit down with colleagues and consider these questions:

1 How does the new student feel and react to everything that happens up to the beginning of the first proper lesson? Arrival, foreign airport, immigration, transfer, host family, getting to new school, first-day procedure ... By the time the first lesson begins, a lot has already happened, and first reactions may have started to set into enduring attitudes, for better or for worse.

2 Do you have a 'welcome pack' – is it valuable? What to include? What about pre-course information, sent by mail? Is it worth the expense? Yes, probably: any *accessible* information is useful and helps reduce fear of the unknown; but not if it is a major comprehension exercise that induces perplexity rather than reassurance. More realistic for many schools is a personal 'welcome letter' – 'Thank you for your booking, we confirm your enrolment in the following course, we look forward to seeing you here on such-and-such a date. If you have any questions or need any more information, don't hesitate to contact me.'

3 Atmosphere and feel – what atmosphere do you want to create? How can you create the atmosphere you want in respect of identifying names and responsibilities of staff, decor and furniture, arrangement of reception area, etc?

4 Most of all, it is *people* that create atmosphere. How do you think students interpret the real 'intention' of the staff? How can you encourage, motivate and inspire staff to give students that special warmth and personal interest? This is not just a question of wanting to be nice: clients of any business will remember a smiling face or a genuine effort to give personal attention, probably long after they remember much about the product or service itself, and will make recommendations on that basis.

● ●

True story *Welcome to Heathrow*

The seventeen-year-old student arrived at the airport after a twelve-hour flight from Japan. There was a long queue at the immigration desk – a twenty-five-minute wait, followed by questions that were difficult to understand, although not hostile. One of the handles of her new suitcase had been broken in transit. The promised taxi was not there to meet her. She waited half an hour, then rehearsing the little English at her command, she changed some money, worked out with the aid of a pocket dictionary how to use the public phone and phoned the school, to get a recorded message giving two emergency numbers. Although she couldn't understand the message fully, she guessed the gist and by listening several times through, she managed to write the numbers down. There was no answer from the first. The second was the home number of the director, who in a flurry of subsequent calls established that the taxi had broken down and that a replacement was on the way. She had to wait another hour in a crowded and confusing airport terminal, in a state of considerable anxiety, until the relief driver picked her up. Fortunately, the host family had been warned of the delay, and were sympathetic and welcoming. On the Monday morning, when asked how she was feeling after her experience, she replied 'I feel so old.'

● ●

2 How do you make placement decisions and when do you change them?

Which class a student is placed in is probably the single most crucial decision for successful learning and student satisfaction. It takes time for new students to get to know each other and to get used to the teacher, and for the class as a whole to 'gel'. The more class changes you have to make, the more disruptive it is, especially when there are changes of coursebook or timetable involved as well. You therefore want to make your initial placements as accurately as possible, and to minimize subsequent class changes. How?

The conventional wisdom is that you give new students a test to determine their level, then place them in the class nearest that level. The immediate problems with 'conventional wisdom' are:

- Does the test match what you are teaching? For example, a simple multiple-choice test is inappropriate for what is being taught in classes that emphasize spoken communication.
- A really thorough test of all language skills would take hours, and be uneconomic to administer on a large scale.
- Tests, by their nature, usually inhibit people from showing the best they can do.
- There are other important criteria to bear in mind for placement – see the table below. These are broad generalizations that may be grossly unfair to individual students, but as a mental checklist, they can still be useful.
- In reality, there is rarely an absolutely correct placement – the best decision is a compromise affected by these various factors, and, of course, the range of classes or courses available.

Different criteria...	... and their implications for placement
Length of course	More time to learn thoroughly on a longer course – place lower
Nationality	Mix nationalities as far as possible; strive to avoid one nationality or mother tongue being dominant. Be cautious of stereotypes about particular nationalities; but they are often true
Educational background	More experience of studying: place higher
Motivation	Strong immediate motivation – eg job promotion, more money – place up
Age	Generally, older people learn more slowly (but not less well) than younger people. Place lower, less loss of face if younger classmates overtake (but beware of unconscious ageism!)
Personality	High self-esteem and confidence are arguably the most important factors in successful language learning. Place up for both; unless they are combined with low self-awareness, in which case you have a problem! Place lower the naturally shy or taciturn
Personal choice	Invite the student to express a preference!

Some general placement tips:

- If in doubt, place down rather than up.
- If all other things are equal, invite the student to choose.
- Avoid making changes within four to six lessons unless someone is clearly misplaced.
- 'Talk to your teacher first.' As the first line of class management, the teacher must be consulted immediately; if the student is reluctant to do so, then the course director/director of studies must seek the teacher's opinion.
- Be as open as possible about your reasons for not making changes, eg doubts about suitability of level or lack of space.

See also 'How do you test and place students on short courses?' in Chapter 7, Section 5, p 143.

Some non-linguistic but quite genuine reasons for wanting to change class:

The hours suit me better, I have football practice on Thursdays.

My friend is in that class.

You must not put me in that class. He is junior to me.

I want to be in the same class as Claudia.

I don't want to be in the same class as Erik. Not any more. Not after last week.

If you put me in a lower class, it will take me longer to reach the target level for my grade, and I would far rather be here in the training centre than back at work.

Class size and mixed levels: can you ever get it right?

For a given number of students, the *more you place in fewer classes:*

- the more 'mixed' the levels of the classes are likely to be;
- the fewer teachers you will need, so:
- the more profitable that course will be in the short term, but:
- the more likely you are to have dissatisfied students (and teachers), so:
- the greater the risk of long-term deterioration of quality and business.

On the other hand, the *fewer you place in more classes:*

- the more finely-tuned the levels will be, in theory at least;
- the more teachers you will need;
- the less profitable that course is likely to be, so:
- the more likely that you will eventually have to increase the price, and in doing so:
- the more likely you will risk pricing it too high and running out of students.

How price-sensitive are your clients? Can they see the benefits of small classes? Do your students generally agree that it's worth paying more for smaller classes? Ask them, informally or by a marketing survey.

Is it a heresy to suggest that in fact students can be perfectly happy and learn just as much in mixed-level classes? There is a risk that we place our own professional judgement above the decisions made by students about how to spend their money. Whether a class is considered to be 'mixed-level' is itself largely a value-judgement. It depends on:

1 The syllabus. The more pre-determined and structured the syllabus is, the more likely it is that there will be problems with different abilities and interests. If it is based on a step-by-step system of linear increments, the wider the distribution of existing 'states of knowledge' in the class, the more frustration will result.

2 The methodology. Again, the more tightly-constrained the range of activities and patterns of interaction possible in the class, the more likely it is that the teacher will have to teach to the 'middle ground' and leave the strongest to get bored and the weakest behind.

3 The teacher. Most importantly, **experienced teachers cope much better with mixed-level classes**, and can exploit them successfully and enjoyably. It would be surprising if this were not the case.

3 How do you increase non-teaching revenue?

(You could usefully do this as a group activity, informally with a small group of colleagues.)

1 Identify your assets and resources, eg from the strategy formulation activity (Chapter 2, Section 4, pp 24–30).
2 Look down the list of ideas for generating extra revenue on pp 111–12 . Pick two or three possible candidates for further consideration. For each one:
3 Sketch out the local demand for that service. Who would be using such a service now? Who might become users in the near future?
4 Find out what other companies are charging locally for similar services (a couple of quick phone calls may be all that is needed).
5 Direct cost: how much would it cost immediately to provide the service? In terms of staff, equipment, advertising, materials, resources.
6 Indirect costs: work out roughly how much extra administrative work would be generated, eg for reception staff, accounts, cleaners, etc who would not be in the front line, but whose workload would still increase. Setting up a new service takes up a lot of management and administration time even before it produces any revenue. Estimate by what proportion bills for communications and services might be increased, particularly telephone, fax and postage, but also cleaning, light and heat, porterage and security.
7 Work out what you would need to charge to cover direct costs, indirect costs, and to generate a surplus. Be realistic. What is the minimum surplus that would make it worth doing? Do you want to be a 'busy fool' (see p 111), creating a lot of extra work that generates little extra income?

> **What is a 'busy fool'?** – a person who works industriously to conceive, plan, implement and develop a project that makes little profit. It is easy to fall into the 'every little bit helps' trap without being honest with yourself about the true cost: although the management time may cost nothing extra in terms of immediate expenditure, it is still a real cost, because it is time spent on this project that cannot be spent on another.

True story   *Keyboard skills*

It seemed a good idea at the time. There were a lot of young Japanese women students who were learning English on a long-term basis, many of whom would be using it in a secretarial capacity when they got home. Why not offer a typing course? – one hour a day after school. The school secretary was a highly competent and trained typist, who could buy a couple of typing coursebooks, then develop and teach a short typing course. The manager whose idea it was spent a lot of time visiting office machinery shops comparing features and prices, and proudly came home with a taxi full of machines on special offer (there was a free fountain pen with every one).

The students were recruited internally (a free fountain pen being offered to the first five who enrolled), the course got under way, and went very successfully. In terms of direct costs, the cost of the machines was paid off and as the staffing was already being paid for, it showed a profit.

In terms of indirect costs, the school secretary had to spend a considerable amount of time preparing to teach the course, as she had no previous instructional experience; she had be covered while teaching the course, which meant that at times the office was under considerable pressure, and that at other times a senior manager came in to answer the phones. Well, why not?

The typewriters are still there, much used by teaching staff to type out worksheets and other teaching materials. Even though the initial investment in equipment has already been made, somehow there doesn't seem to be the enthusiasm for repeating the exercise.

COMMENT: The decision to proceed with the idea was essentially one person's. It was probably not a bad decision, but neither was it part of a longer-term strategy. A lot of work went into it, but not a lot of thought.

Ideas for generating extra revenue

Things you can charge for
- for coursebooks;
- other schools and companies for teacher recruitment;
- a registration/enrolment fee;
- consider making a nominal charge if you offer free lessons as part of teacher-training programmes.

Things you can sell

- books and learning materials; stationery, confectionery, T-shirts (with or without school logo!);
- accommodation services;
- guiding in English/foreign languages for tourists/business visitors;
- travel services, eg train, bus or parking tickets;
- language travel-related insurance services;
- transfer services between airport/sea port/railway/bus station and school/host family; or negotiate more favourable bulk terms with local taxi companies;
- produce distance-learning materials/correspondence courses to sell to students, company clients and/or publishers;

Extra services you can offer

- develop cultural awareness training;
- create spectacular events and activities so good that students don't mind paying extra (eg musical events and performances by English-through-theatre groups);
- offer translation and/or interpreting services;
- proof-read for authors and publishers;
- set up as an examination centre;
- set up a language travel agency, selling courses at other schools;
- set up and service self-access centres, eg for companies;
- set up catering services, or rent the catering facilities out, or put a catering contract out to tender (don't forget to set performance criteria).

Financial arrangements

- review your system and application of cancellation fees;
- arrange with your bank for all credit surpluses above a certain level to be transferred immediately and automatically to an interest-bearing account;
- install pay telephones if tariffs are favourable; sell telephone cards (credit card phones may be particularly attractive for international calls);
- hire out rooms;
- offer students a quick and convenient photo developing service;
- install juke box, video games.

4 How do you manage teaching resources?

Books

You should be able to negotiate a discount of 5–15 per cent from a bookshop in return for a promise of regular custom. For major course start dates, when you know you will need a large of number of new coursebooks but won't know which until you have tested all the students, try to negotiate a 'sale or return' basis. You could consider setting up your own school bookshop as an extra source of revenue; even a small display can bring in a regular small sum.

There are various options for costing the use of a coursebook. You can:

- give it (ie include cost in the tuition fee);
- charge an extra flat fee for teaching materials, books included;
- sell it at retail cost, generating a small extra income (so some students will pay more than others for their book);
- lend it ('please don't write in it: give back at the end of the course or when you change class').

Alternatively, you can avoid using coursebooks. Ask yourself a basic question to start from: What is the fundamental rationale for using a coursebook in your institution? Do all the students really need one? Will your teaching staff make enough use of it? Is it replaceable as a 'psychological prop'? Are there classes or groups who either have their own very specific material or who will in reality end up using bits and pieces from a lot of different sources?

Hardware

Purchase over a period of time on 'easy payment' terms or 'lease purchase' is much easier on the cash-flow than outright purchase, but beware of getting locked into long contracts that appear initially attractive but could become millstones. This commonly happens in the UK with photocopiers and vending machines – it is often worth paying more for the flexibility of maximum one-year contracts.

In general, for equipment such as cassette recorders for use by a number of different people, avoid the state of the art in preference for the tried and tested. Compare price and performance for:

- professional standard – very expensive, very high quality, high security risk; compared to:
- 'classroom machines' – specially designed and built for classroom use; more robust, more durable, more expensive, better sound quality for larger rooms, less likely to be stolen, more likely to be reparable; compared to:
- domestic – cheap, more easily available, regard as consumable – may not be worth repairing when they break down.

In general, buy the most simple that meet your requirements – there are fewer things to go wrong, and it will be easier for people to learn to use them properly.

Don't forget training sessions, or at least clear written instructions, for new machines. Get one or two staff to read the manual thoroughly, try them out in class, then report back to other staff on how best to use them.

Furniture

How long will students be sitting on the chairs in class? Hard plastic or wood may be bearable for an hour or two, but not four or five hours a day!

Do you want to equip your classrooms with one big central table, small tables/desks, or chairs with 'tablet' arms? The choice depends on the atmosphere you want to create, and the most common class activities. Tables are better for a lot of writing and exam work; one big central table creates a more business-like 'boardroom' feel; individual chairs with writing arms are better for communication activities. Small tables for two or three people offer a lot of flexibility and are easily moved around. Folding chairs *can* be comfortable, and can have folding writing arms.

When you've decided what you want, shop around. Particularly with specific furniture requirements, it is worth spending quite a lot of time checking out different suppliers. Try also contacting manufacturers directly; get on the mailing lists of auction rooms and specialist suppliers, for example of educational equipment. Always keep your eye open when visiting other schools and colleges – if you see something you like, ask who their supplier is.

Utilization

In a traditional school, most of the space is taken up by classrooms, which are only in use a certain number of hours on certain days, but not in breaks, at lunchtime, after school, evenings or weekends. Yet this space is a major overhead cost: you pay to rent it, heat it, light it, clean it, tax it and so on. Why not look for ways to increase the utilization?

As a first step, work out how many hours a week your major rooms are actually used. Include language laboratories, lounges and meeting rooms as well as classrooms. Which of them are the most under-utilized?

Work through your class records to compare class sizes with room sizes. For example, you might find that your classrooms can hold fourteen students, but the advertised maximum group size is twelve and the average class size is only nine students. Obviously, you can put the larger classes in the larger rooms for comfort; but also if your average class size is quite a bit less than your advertised maximum, you are losing out on the potential selling point of small classes. On the other hand, if the existing premises are a major constraint on class size, and if internal alterations or being able to rent one or two classrooms nearby might bring the class average significantly nearer to the stated maximum, you can improve profitability.

Is there any scope for *multi-purpose flexibility* – eg using a room as a lounge at lunchtime, and a classroom at peak lesson times? Or an office in low season as a small or one-to-one classroom in high season? Or the language laboratory as a self-access/listening centre after class hours?

Would a shift system help utilization where the schedule for a particular course is quoted as, for example, 'three hours per day morning or afternoon' or '4–6 pm or 6–8 pm depending on level'? Particularly for holiday classes or peak season courses, it is possible to make a positive feature of a shift system. Different hours often suit different groups of people such as evening workers, commuters or students; there is usually better access to other facilities such as sports in the morning for holiday course students in afternoon classes. If there is a strong preference for one timetable, eg mornings, you can alternate morning and afternoon classes week by week to make the distribution as fair as possible and to give variety.

In the longer term, you can also manipulate price differentials to encourage less popular schedules. For example, the Monday/Wednesday evening classes might be made a little cheaper than the Tuesday/Thursday evenings because a historical analysis shows that they are traditionally harder to fill. This is just a variation of 'lower prices in low season, higher prices in high season' based on a shorter time-cycle.

Security

If you are very lucky, you live and work in a place where security is not a major headache. For the rest of us, it is a concern that constantly influences the selection, deployment and use of our premises and resources. There are many positive steps that can be taken to reduce or prevent theft and loss.

Ideas for improving the security of premises and resources:

Mark it
- Stamp books immediately on purchase with the school name and address. If theft is a serious problem, stamp in several places in the text of the book wherever there is space, eg the last page of a chapter or unit. Clip the corner off the cover.
- Number class sets of books. For serious problems, have a resources person/librarian check them out and in; teachers sign. This is tedious but effective.
- For hardware, paint the school name and address with indelible marker or special anti-theft paint. Don't be afraid to paint all over – a lurid machine is more use than a missing one.
- Buy or borrow an etching kit to mark machines with postcode and/or phone number. Use paint to emphasize this.
- Make an immediate record of all serial and model numbers, together with date and place of purchase, and record the location of the equipment in the school. Check this list every two or three months and update it.

Fix it
- Get special cabinets to mount videos in, which are too heavy to carry out. This is expensive but worth it in the long run.
- Get expensive fixed equipment bolted into the wall or floor. Label it to show that forced removal will destroy the machine.
- Create a strongroom in which all valuable equipment is stored overnight. This is obviously the first room you should install an alarm in.

Alarms
- Alarm systems: get advice about the local suitability of various features that are available, eg do you want audible warning? How much would it cost to be connected to a central station: is it worth paying the extra? How are the police to be alerted if the alarm goes off? Bear in mind that an alarm has a primarily deterrent function; it is better to keep intruders out than have the alarm go off when they've already got in.
- Anti-tilt video alarms are cheap and quite effective against walk-in theft.
- Install a fixed equipment alarm system, where the machines are wired together.

Keys
- Plan carefully any security system that relies on keys. Number them and keep an up-to-date list of who has which keys. Keys are small and easily lost, especially when passed from person to person regularly. Plan a back-up system for when the vital key is lost or the keyholder is unexpectedly delayed or absent.
- Restricted keys – can only be cut against authorized signature.

Personal

- Issue cards and get students to show them on entry, which may be especially worthwhile with large numbers of part-time students whose faces may not all be familiar.
- Find out about awareness training courses for your staff. A large amount of crime against businesses is opportunistic, and can be prevented by alert staff knowing what to look out for and how to react.

5   How do you build/develop a self-access centre?

Definition: a self-access centre is a resource of learning materials to which students can have direct access, without the mediation of a teacher or other member of staff.

The first question to ask is: Is it worth it? The arguments for self-access centres are essentially educational. Some students don't like them and prefer not to use them, unless they are scheduled into the programme. If you are thinking of setting up such a centre, you therefore need to ask yourself what you want a self-access centre for. It's useful to draw up a list of your priorities. For example:

- to promote learner independence;
- to fill gaps in the syllabus or programme, eg to allow classes to concentrate on certain areas;
- to meet individual specific needs;
- to provide further low-cost language practice;
- to offer greater variety for learning;
- to generate income – usually the use of a·self-access centre is included in the fees, but you can also charge on a subscription or per use basis.

How will it be used?

These options are not necessarily exclusive:

- It can be scheduled into the class timetable: classes in rotation, once a day or two or three times a week, with the regular class teacher in attendance to direct students toward specific gaps in their skills that she knows need particular practice.
- It can be available on a open-booking basis, for a teacher to decide to spend a lesson or part of a lesson in the centre to work on some particular skill or material.
- It can be an optional extra hour at the end of the day for students from any class.
- It can be available at other free times, eg before classes in the morning, during lunch break, at weekends.
- It can operate as a work-in centre only, or as a borrowing facility with the possibility of taking materials away, eg study material, readers, listening tapes, videos.

What will it contain?

There are many possible sources of material:

- published EFL self-access material;
- published EFL class textbooks, adapted as necessary (eg drills and listening exercises);
- non-EFL educational materials, eg for secondary schools, or company-sponsored educational materials;
- authentic materials, adapted;
- authentic materials, raw (including newspapers, magazines, TV);
- home-made materials.

The table below comments on specific materials from different sources. Don't forget to check copyright rules to see whether you have the right to copy a piece of material freely, for use within an institution, or not at all.

Self-access centre: materials	
Materials	**Comment**
Coursebooks and supplementary books	Students may have met them before They may not be 'learner-friendly' without the teacher's book
Listening cassettes in general	Popular; level of difficulty not immediately obvious, so level-coding may be needed Expensive to make and replace
Pronunciation activities	Often very popular; really need AAC facility (audio-active comparative, so students can listen, speak/record, rewind and compare)
Dictation	Popular; lots of different possibilities Level-coding may be needed
Recorded news bulletins (audio/video)	Labour-intensive to prepare worksheets but topical and popular
Authentic materials	Attractive to the eye, but language level often too high; they may need a lot of work to adapt for wider use, and may date quickly
All home-made materials	Can be focused to needs, but labour-intensive to produce to a high standard and expensive to make them look good
Reference books	Often needs someone to point students towards suitable books and encourage use
Readers (EFL publishers' series)	Popular: can they be borrowed? Will security be a problem?
Computers: EFL software	An increasing range available. Popular, but educational value-for-money still open to debate
Computers: other applications (look at 'shareware' especially)	Word-processing useful for projects; all kinds of possibilities for self-directed project work There is an increasing range of 'edutainment' software which offers a lot of language practice

How will it be presented and maintained?

Which development route do you want to take? The showpiece multi-media centre where requirements can be anticipated and a lot of expensive development work is done in advance before it opens with a fanfare; or the 'softly softly' route that starts with a bare minimum, but is able to produce materials quickly to meet particular demands? These two options are extremes, and in most cases the development route will fall between the two; how far along the scale between the two extremes it is will influence strongly how it can be presented to students.

Image and packaging

How important is the 'corporate identity' of your school or institution? Do you want standard folders and files with logo, colour and other codes? It may cost more to set up, but once done, it looks good and gives new students an immediate impression of good organization.

Location

It doesn't have to be a huge multi-media room:

- You can use the language laboratory as a self-access listening centre (experience shows that students working on their own very often prefer precisely the kind of listening exercises that are out of favour in class, eg pronunciation drills and mechanical dictation exercises).
- You can use a lounge as a comfortable reading room.
- You can use spare classrooms for intensive reading and writing work; speaking with a portalab (shy or low level students may be more willing to experiment if they are not being overheard); project work with small groups.
- You can use office space and equipment by arrangement, eg typewriter, computer, telephone. The internal telephone system is particularly useful for authentic telephone skills practice, and it's free!
- You can use the TV lounge/video room for scheduled TV/video programmes.
- You can also use a library or quiet room for TV/video by wiring in sets of headphones to a simple junction box so as not to disturb others.
- At its most minimal, a self-access centre can be a cupboard open at certain times for material to be loaned and taken away.

You need to consider how to enable students to make the most of the facility. You could orientate them in groups at the beginning of each course: individually, by the teacher for a new student; or remotely, by an explanatory leaflet or tape, ideally in their own language, that explains the various features and how best to use them.

Organization

How will the material be indexed? You may want to use different coding systems for different types of material, and/or develop a cross-reference system held in a central index. You can index:

- by **skill**: eg listening/speaking/reading/writing, then sub-skills, eg speaking broken down into pronunciation/intonation/stress/dialogue repetition/transformation and substitution drills;
- by **topic**: eg business can be broken down as finely as required, into banking/management/marketing/accounting;
- by **level** (is it necessary?) Keep it simple, to three or four levels, perhaps colour-coded; with authentic materials, it is the activity that should be indexed by level, not the material itself;
- by **language area**: grammatical structure/function/lexis.

As a general rule, keep the structure simple so that it is easy to use, but also make it flexible so that it can accommodate future developments.

Syllabus link

What link is there with other courses and to the rest of the curriculum? Do you want to keep it separate, or to encourage teachers to refer students to particular skills and activities in the self-access centre, and encourage students to take responsibility for their own learning by reflecting on their own strengths, weaknesses and particular needs, and using the self-access centre accordingly?

Support and maintenance

Who is going to maintain the facility? Who is responsible for developing and indexing new materials? What budget is there?

- -

True story   *Receiving loud and clear*

The director of studies in charge of language laboratory maintenance at an industrial language training centre was surprised at the enthusiasm shown by the trainee vehicle fitters for extra lab work in the guided self-study period. He was further perplexed to find teeth-marks in most of the headset cables. The technician who came to service the lab provided the explanation – by biting into the cables until their teeth touched the wire inside, the students were able to pick up and listen to music programmes from the powerful local FM radio station.

- -

6   How do you make the 'other eighteen hours' of significant value?

This section is aimed at schools based in native-speaker countries, who recruit 'language travel' students from non-native-speaker countries. In a typical day, a student will be studying for three or four hours; an intensive course might be five or at most six hours. That leaves eighteen hours a day plus weekends! How can you maximize the language-learning opportunities of this time? First of all, why is it desirable? Different theories offer different reasons:

1 Students can only concentrate for so long.
2 Formal learning can only achieve so much, compared to informal acquisition.
3 Learning is important, practice makes perfect.
4 The more we can relax and lower our mental barriers, the more natural language we will be able to take in and reproduce.
5 Comprehensible input is supposed to be the key. But are native speakers comprehensible? Not always!

Ideas for exploiting the language potential of non-teaching hours

- Accommodation – plan how it can be exploited for maximum language practice benefit as well as comfort and value for money – see below.
- Self-access centre – see previous section.
- Lounge – comfortable for conversation; newspapers, magazines, TV; board games, etc.
- Activities and excursions programme – see below.
- Set up simple projects or 'treasure hunts' that require students to navigate their way around, answering questions (without bothering the locals too much). For younger students in particular, such projects offer a way to create interaction between the student and the local community in a carefully controlled way.
- Present students with carefully selected local information: what's on where, how to find your way around. This can save a lot of the time it takes students to familiarize themselves. Do this by wall displays; handouts and orientation sessions on the first day (remember, most spoken orientation is wasted, unless supported by visual or textual information); regular 'what's on' briefings, or visits to classrooms.
- The public library often has a wealth of different resources and things to do. You may need to prepare a separate guide or introductory leaflet to help students make the most of it, if the library doesn't have one already.
- Build bridges. Encourage self-help in the local English-speaking environment by pointing people in the right direction: eg putting them in touch with local clubs (chess, yoga, sports, aerobics, professional groups) to pursue personal interests. Language learned in a context of strong personal interest will be more meaningful and will be retained better.
- Conversation exchange. Spread the word that you will set up such exchanges, get interested parties to advertise on cards on your notice board, encourage them to contact each other.
- Contact local schools and arrange for your students to visit classes learning your students' native language, to talk about their native country and culture, to be used as a native-speaker resource by the teacher. In return, your students get some language practice in English as well as an opportunity to learn about

schools and the education system. For rarer languages, contact adult part-time or evening classes.
- Publicize the requirements of local voluntary groups, who are usually only too keen for volunteers with at least an intermediate level of English to help out, perhaps in a charity shop, for a day or a couple of hours.

The last four suggestions, in particular, are in accord with the general principle of trying to seek ways to contribute to as well as take from the local community.

Projects outside the classroom

('Outside' here means outside in time, outside class hours, as well as outside physically.)

The general model is **prepare** in the class, **carry out** outside, **follow up** and exploit back in the classroom. The execution of the project outside is the shortest stage, taking perhaps only an hour or two. If well planned, which takes time, the project will generate an enormous amount of language discussion and practice in the follow-up stage.

Ideas for project-based work

- Use host families as a major resource. They are, after all, paid to talk to students.
- Use non-teaching staff as a resource (interview, profile, questionnaire).
- Set projects rather than homework – a question of attitude as well as activity.
- Identify and exploit local sources of information such as lending and reference libraries, tourist information offices, schools, sympathetic local businesses, voluntary groups who would welcome students' help.
- Identify project activities that will generate useful information as well as being intrinsic language-learning tasks, eg information about local shops or facilities that other students would find interesting.
- Allow plenty of time to finish off the project properly, with a smart written/typed report and/or an oral presentation. In either case, several drafts/rehearsals may be needed. It is frustrating for students to put a lot of effort into a project then not be able to complete it fully for lack of time.
- Display or make a presentation to other students, as appropriate.
- Use school equipment (typewriter, word-processor, photocopier, etc) to make it look as good as possible. Let students use the equipment themselves if competent, or if time is not pressing; otherwise, get them to explain to the administrative/secretarial staff exactly what they want.
- If possible, give each contributor a copy to take home.

Planning accommodation

Where students are coming to study in a foreign country, or do not live within travelling distance of the course centre, schools typically offer accommodation services. Most commonly these are:

Host family or homestay
where the student is welcomed into a local family, treated by and large as a member of the family, and provided with bed and certain meals on a pre-arranged basis.

Residential

where sleeping accommodation and catering services are offered within or adjacent to the course centre. This may range from a small executive school or country house with a handful of bedrooms (usually all year round) to a large college premises with dormitories for several hundred (usually seasonal).

Guest house or hotel

where the student is a normal paying guest, and the school may only be involved by making the initial recommendation although often schools are able to negotiate a discount on behalf of their students.

The accommodation service may be organized:

- as an integral part of the whole course package, as is typically the case with residential centres;
- as an optional extra, generating a distinct source of profit;
- as an optional extra service to students, on a 'break-even' basis;
- on a 'bought-in' basis, with a freelance homestay agent or consultant paid a fixed fee for each student they place, and some kind of periodic commission to ensure continuing care and service;
- merely as an information service, giving details of local families, guest houses or hotels, and leaving students to make their own arrangements.

This section is principally concerned with host family ('homestay') accommodation because it is the most economical and the most popular of the three options, and because the administration of the homestay programme is usually an integral part of the management concerns of small or medium-sized schools. Residential centres by contrast are usually hired on a seasonal basis with housekeeping, cleaning and catering staff as part of the package; the role of the course manager is liaison rather than administration.

Organization of a homestay programme

Recruitment of homestay families

by advertisement, leafleting, targeted mailing, or best of all, word of mouth.

Inspection visit

and initial acceptance or rejection, making a note of any worries or reservations you may have – use an initial questionnaire/checklist about the house and the family.

Regular re-visit and record-keeping

Family circumstances and atmosphere change; it is important to keep in touch and make regular visits to feel the atmosphere.

Placement process

matching student to family – increasingly, computer-based school administration packages offer searching and selection by multiple criteria, but for the final decision you cannot beat an experienced accommodation/welfare officer with an instinct for the job.

Forward information

Give both parties information about the other – specific details of names, ages, jobs, interests, dietary preferences, allergies, etc. Get both parties to write a short letter or note to the other, if at all possible.

Contract

Make explicit the 'contract' between family and student – letting each know what is expected of them, and what they can expect of the other party. See Chapter 7, Section 2.

Monitoring during the course

This requires a light but sensitive hand; you can use a questionnaire after the student has had time to settle in (ten days to two weeks), but only if you still have the time to act on any strong complaints that emerge. Encourage all staff to act as the eyes and ears of the school – to listen out for and follow up odd comments that students make, to talk to students who appear unhappy and pass on relevant information.

Follow-up and feedback

at the end and after the course – an end-of-course questionnaire is too late to help make any changes for that student, but will help future students. Any strong comments that emerge should be considered carefully and followed up: the first step being to hear both sides of the story! A phone call to the family allows them to express their reactions to the student, and allows you to make better placement decisions in future. Although an individual student's comments may be highly personal and idiosyncratic, over a period of time you will build up a clearer and more reliable picture of each family, and which kind of students they are most successful and happy with.

It is important that you not only *tell* your families what services and facilities you expect them to provide, but that you know they have *understood and agreed* to this contract. You therefore need a written leaflet or list of points to give them; maybe you should have a 'sign and return' slip indicating their understanding and acceptance of the details. You might also want to produce a leaflet covering the same points for your students, so they know what to expect. The more detail you can settle in advance, the more confident and relaxed both parties will be in their relationship.

Like so many tasks involving the management of people, this one is essentially about striking the right balance between helping students make the most of their course by smoothing out potential problems and misunderstandings, without going so far that you remove any need for students to use their initiative and their newly-acquired command of the language to help themselves. 'Over-counselling' is the stage at which the student comes to you to ask you to make a perfectly ordinary and mundane request to the host family, rather than approaching them directly.

7 How do you plan an activities and excursions programme?

First of all, what are the advantages and disadvantages of offering a programme of extra activities?

Advantages	Disadvantages
It provides opportunities for language practice with native or other non-native speakers in a relaxed, non-classroom, 'not on show' environment, where the normal rules of conversation operate, rather than 'teacher' rules; but at the same time where there is usually a high tolerance of hesitation and error.	There is a risk of coddling: a full, varied, well-organized activities and excursions programme can make it virtually unnecessary for the unadventurous to attempt to penetrate the local community on their own, except through mediation of the school: family, activity, the excursion are all set up for them. This is the package holiday syndrome: can it become counter-productive for real-life language acquisition and practice? Does it matter?
Relaxation and pleasure are an important and growing part of the 'language travel' package. People need variety.	People have increasingly high expectations of leisure services and facilities; to the extent that students are tourists, they may expect tourist services of a professional standard.
It makes better use of the student's limited time. It informs the individual about the host culture, which ultimately enables him/her to exploit it better and to learn and use its language more meaningfully.	Students are likely to be less perceptive about the use of language and about aspects of culture if they are in a larger group of foreign students rather than in a small group or on their own.
It provides a rich source of experience to discuss and exploit in class (not just 'What did you do at the weekend?' but 'What differences in ... have you noticed between here and your country? Why do you think these differences exist?' etc).	The potential for exploitation in class is greater if the students have had different experiences at the weekend or the evening before, rather than having all been to the same place on the same trip.
It can generate income.	It can take a lot of organizing for little or no extra income, particularly when your student numbers are low.

An activities and excursions programme can be offered as an integral part of a whole package – typically for junior courses and some adult package holiday courses; or as an optional extra, which students can choose to participate in or not as they choose. It can be provided 'in-house' by staff contracted to organize and deliver a specified programme; or it can be 'bought in' from freelance external contractors who undertake to offer an agreed minimum standard of programme, and to charge fees within a specified range. Alternatively it can be a mixture of the two, where a social manager is employed part-time for a basic salary to provide an agreed basic programme of free and cheap social activities, and also buys services in or runs an income-generating excursion tours business as a sideline, selling directly to the school's students. The excursion budget should include allowances for transport (eg coach hire, parking, tip for driver); entrances (staff as well as students); daily or hourly rate for accompaniers; plus a float for emergencies.

Some possible activities

Evenings at school

- club evenings at the school, making use of existing recreational facilities (table tennis, snooker, computer games, karaoke, board games, music, television, etc); organized competitions;
- video evenings, showing feature films. An interval allows people to stretch their legs and have some refreshment, also for a member of staff to answer any questions about language comprehension!
- national evenings (song, dance, food, etc prepared and presented by students from a particular country);
- welcome and goodbye parties. At welcome parties new students can be introduced by name; at farewell parties you can hand out certificates, etc, or just say goodbye (with lots of taking photographs and exchanging addresses).

Evening events outside school

- visits to theatre, cinema and concert;
- any special local events, festivals and celebrations.

Sports

- team games can be organized in the local park or on the beach – football, netball, rounders, stoolball, etc. Beyond the cost of the basic equipment, such games are enjoyable and cheap;
- court games, such as tennis and squash, can also be organized quite economically, by shopping around to find the best deal and negotiating a block booking discount;
- a package of 'multisports' can be organized with a local sports or fitness club, comprising an economical and enjoyable mixture of badminton, table tennis, five-a-side football, fitness circuit, etc;
- special features, eg riding, ice-skating, roller-skating, wind-surfing, etc;
- crazy games: 'egg and spoon' type races, crazy golf, etc.

True story   *No more churches*

The teacher was describing the next day's activities in enthusiastic terms. Ingvar, one of the Icelandic boys, asked 'Are there any castles or churches on this trip?' 'Well, yes, in fact there is a beautiful cathedral which we will visit in the morning.' 'Oh no, not another church. I have seen more churches in the last three weeks than in my whole life. Please, no more churches!'

As well as the obvious famous towns and historic sights, excursions can be arranged to:

- theme parks (especially for juniors/teenagers). The initial cost of entry is usually high, but there is lots to do after that, and plenty of choice. It is often best to programme this for a midweek if possible, so that less time spent in queues;
- commercial premises that offer tours: a biscuit factory, a car body plant, a brewery or distillery (eg for students of professional or business English);
- sports events: as well as the obvious tennis, football, baseball, cricket, it is usually possible to arrange one or two more specialized choices such as horse-racing, motor-racing, ice-hockey, etc.

Some other ideas:

- Offer one 'special' event, perhaps more expensive than the rest, but something that students will remember for a long time: eg a special theatre or musical show, or a visit to a Disney-type theme park. Find out what special events would really interest students, then try to get special rates by early/block booking or midweek/matinee booking.
- 'Fulfil your dream' – offer each student the opportunity to spend an evening doing whatever they would really like, but would have been unwilling to attempt on their own, in the company of a member of staff.
- Offer a limited choice of options within the same budget, and get students to discuss and vote.
- As well as informal feedback, give a detailed questionnaire at the end of the course to get comments on each excursion. If you have a predictable pattern of ages and nationalities at different times, work out what each nationality's or group's likes and dislikes are. Anyone for shopping?
- Within the realms of the feasible, try to offer something for everybody. Watch out for the content of the activities programme being influenced, if not actually dictated, by the interests of teachers and/or group leaders!

See also Chapter 7, Section 6, 'Managing activities and excursions at local centres'.

Chapter 7   Managing short courses

Introduction

Most schools and EFL organizations operate some form of 'short course' in addition to their year-round scheduled courses. The umbrella term of 'short courses' is used to refer to a variety of different types of courses including:

- junior residential and host family vacation courses;
- adult residential and host family vacation courses;
- multi-activity vacation courses;
- vacation courses for older and retired age groups;
- specialized vacation courses, eg tourism, golf, literature, riding, etc;
- in-company teaching contracts;
- tailor-made courses, eg ESP courses;
- contracts, eg government training contracts and contracts with large organizations or companies.

The features that distinguish these types of courses from year-round scheduled courses are:

- They tend to be short in duration, anything from a weekend or one week to six months.
- They may be quoted and managed as an all-inclusive package which includes education, accommodation and other services.
- They may require the recruitment of short-term or specialized staff.
- They may involve dealing with one or many groups of students with very particular needs.
- They may entail dealing with intermediaries, ie group leaders.
- They may involve hiring external facilities and premises and arranging visits and transport.

Clearly the distinction between managing so-called 'short courses' and year-round courses is less apparent when the short course extends or is renewed over a long period. For example, an off-site contract for military personnel will rapidly begin to operate more like an annexe of the year-round school after continuing for nine months or a year. However the initial planning and setting-up of the contract will have similarities with preparing a four-week vacation course.

The major model discussed in this chapter is based on the finding, setting up and management of a junior residential and host family centre which caters for individuals and groups. Many of the issues and factors looked at are, for the most part, applicable to other types of short courses.

1 Finding a centre

What do you look for?

There are a number of conditions that must be satisfied when looking for a suitable venue for your course:

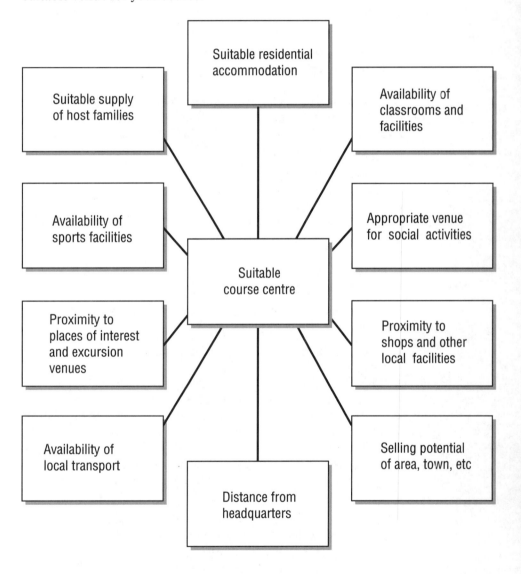

For each of these factors you can construct a simple checklist of questions you will want to ask in order to determine the overall suitability of the venue (see pp 129–130).

Assessing the suitability of a centre – checklists

Host families

Is there a sufficient supply of suitable host families?

What percentage are within walking distance of the venue?

Are you competing for the supply of host families with other organizations?

What is the going rate for host families in the area?

Are the host family source areas and other areas students may travel through pleasant and safe?

Local transport

Are there regular public transport services between the families and the centre?

How long will the journey take for each student?

What time is the last bus or train home in the evening for host family students?

Are there regular transport services to and from other facilities?

Are weekly or monthly tickets available and how much are they?

Residential accommodation

Are shared and single rooms available?

What percentage are shared and single?

How many share a room?

Do the rooms have wash basins?

Are there adequate washing and toilet facilities?

What is the ratio of showers, baths and toilets to rooms?

Who allocates rooms to students?

What cleaning is included in the price per night?

What is the standard of decoration and furbishment?

How far is the accommodation from other facilities?

What are the exact dates all the rooms are available?

Other facilities

Are there any public telephones available?

Are there any relaxation areas or TV lounges, etc?

What laundry, ironing and self-catering facilities are available?

Meals

How many meals can be provided?

How many courses for each meal?

Are sample menus available?

What is the standard of food supplied?

Are hygiene, fire and safety regulations adhered to?

Are packed lunches available?

Is the refectory close to the accommodation?

Safety and security

How secure are the rooms, the accommodation blocks/houses and the campus?

Is the accommodation supervised at night?

Does the centre have public liability and other necessary insurances?

Financial considerations

What is expected in terms of breakages, damage, etc?

What is the rate for accommodation and/or meals?

What does the nightly or weekly rate include and not include?

Classrooms and other facilities

How many classrooms are available?

How many students do the classrooms comfortably hold?

Do they have white or black boards?

Do the students sit at tables and chairs or do they use flap study chairs?

Are OHPs, videos, cameras, computers, etc available for use?

Are the classrooms cleaned regularly?

What are the exact dates the rooms/facilities are available?

What are the rates for room and other equipment hire?

Are there rooms available as offices?

Do you have access to a telephone/fax?

Sports facilities

What local sports are available?

What is their proximity to the centre?

Is tuition available for specialist sports?

Are high-risk sports adequately supervised?

Do sports suppliers have the necessary insurance?

What dates and times are facilities available?

What are the costs for the hire of sports facilities?

Activities – venues and facilities

Are there relaxation areas and snack bar facilities available at the centre?

What rooms are available for activities?

What type of activities would be acceptable to the centre?

Is there a students' union organization or other facilities which may be of use?

Is there a minibus available for hire?

What are the rates for the hire of rooms and other facilities?

Are there any hidden costs such as caretaker costs?

The local area

What are the selling points of the centre, the locality and surrounding area?

Are shops, banks, post office and other amenities within easy reach?

What are the travelling distances and costs to airports or ports?

How far is the centre from your administrative headquarters?

Places of interest and excursion venues

What local places of interest could feature in your programme?

What sights and attractions are within travelling distance?

What local clubs and societies are there and how could they be utilized to add something different to the programme?

Are there any local entertainers, craftspeople, historians or musicians who could contribute to the programme?

What are the costs of sights, attractions and your travel to and from them?

Do attractions offer group rates or discounts at certain times?

Having done your market research you will hopefully have a picture in your mind of the residential requirements of your potential clients. You should, for example, be clear about what type of overall centre you are looking for. You may be seeking a campus situation with all facilities on site or residential accommodation within walking or reasonable travelling distance of the classrooms and day centre.

Very often the difficulty of finding appropriate residential accommodation or good local transport will dictate the location of your centre. There is little point in having a superior centre which is so badly located that students are unable to travel comfortably to and from their host families. If you are not looking for residential accommodation you may be able to choose an area, town or city and find a suitable centre within a matter of weeks but if you require residential accommodation you may be looking at many months or very much longer to complete your research, visit each possibility, negotiate rates and actually confirm a booking.

The focus of your investigation and the questions you want to address will alter if you have any special requirements. For example you may be looking for a locality and hotel conference centre within that locality to provide a language-based management training course for company personnel which is tailored to their very precise requirements. On the other hand you may be looking for a centre with specific technical on-site facilities to manage a six-month ESP contract. Whatever your reason for seeking a centre you have to be clear what your requirements are. In the case of a contract course your client needs analysis should provide a clear centre profile for you to base your search upon. With a planned vacation centre for scheduled courses you will need to do some market research with agents and other sources of students to discover what level of take-up you can expect in the first year. Your needs analysis and market research must be comprehensive if your clients are to be satisfied with the course venue. You may find what you consider to be the ideal centre but however good it is in terms of facilities and accommodation it will not sell itself.

- -

True story   *The ideal centre*

The search had been on for over a year and the staff were pleased when the centre of their choice eventually agreed to work with them. The centre had growth potential, superb facilities, an interesting location, and the beds and classrooms were the right price. Unfortunately it was too late to publicize the centre in the brochure for the following year or sell it at the main trade workshops but the staff knew there was a real market demand for this type of centre and with the help of a hurriedly put together special brochure for agents and students they signed the contract and set up the course.

RESULT: Most agents had completed their own brochures and decided which centres they would offer that year. Take-up was so low the course had to be cancelled and severe penalty cancellation fees paid to the college.

- -

How do you successfully negotiate centre and facility prices?

As with all negotiations, your success or failure will probably be directly related to your level of preparation. You should be fully armed with a list of points to make, answers to questions and some ideas which may ease the negotiation and ensure you secure the centre and facilities you want at the lowest possible price:

Preparation

- What is the going rate for such facilities?
- What condition are the facilities in?
- What kind of clients and students would the centre prefer?
- What can you afford? What is your upper limit?
- What guarantees can you realistically agree to?
- What competition is there for the facilities?
- What are the set rates for the facilities?
- What price is the centre hoping to get?
- What references can you offer from other centres, the bank, etc?
- What do you have to offer that others cannot?

Negotiation

- Which rate is most advantageous to you – hourly, nightly, weekly, etc?
- Can you get single rooms for the same price as doubles and trebles, etc?
- Does the rate include or exclude government taxes?
- Can you get free places for staff, group leaders or students?
- Is there a discount for juniors, groups, volume, educational bookings, etc?
- Do you have to guarantee numbers? If so what is the minimum?
- Does the rate include basic maintenance and adequate cleaning?
- Does the rate include the use of relaxation rooms and public areas?
- Can non-residential students use the facilities?
- Can costs be reduced by a sensible reduction of service, eg catering?
- Is it possible to provide packed lunches on occasions?
- Would half-board at weekends be advantageous?
- Are caretaker costs included in the room rates?
- Are there cheap rate dates, times or days?
- If a deposit is required what is the lowest amount and latest date by which it has to be paid?
- Is there a payment schedule and is it negotiable?

Confirmation

If you are unable to achieve agreement on prices it may be useful to suspend negotiations briefly and continue at a later date with a written proposal. Once agreement is reached it is important to ensure that the details of the agreement are written and confirmed between both parties.

Many centres and residences use some form of standard contract and very often these contracts include items or conditions that are inappropriate or irrelevant to the agreement you have arrived at verbally. The centre conference officer, hotelier or bursar may be well aware that the contract does not directly relate to your agreement or that it contains conditions which you would be unable to meet but, in the absence of any formal alternative, they send it to you in the hope you will sign it. There are various ways of dealing with this type of situation:

- Ignore the contract and confirm your agreement in writing.
- Offer a more relevant or appropriate contract.
- Sign the contract but add a sheet of amendments to it.

It will depend on your relationship with the college staff and your judgement of the importance of their contract as to which line of action you take.

Whatever facilities you are booking and negotiating you should develop a good working relationship with your contact at the centre as soon as possible since your future negotiations and security of use will depend to a large degree on this relationship. Your willingness to act in the event of operational problems once the centre is running, and your co-operation and level of communication with centre staff may be overriding factors if, for example, a competitor offers the centre higher guaranteed numbers or a higher rate per person for the following year. Similarly, if you have cash flow difficulties and wish to postpone payment of an invoice or find you cannot meet your agreed numbers, the fact that you explain the situation and remain in constant communication with the centre will often be sufficient to secure their agreement.

True story *A twelve-year relationship*

The college had been publicized in the school's brochure for over twelve years. In fact it was one of the first residential colleges they had worked with. The relationship had developed over the years with a number of different conference officers. Another new conference officer was appointed and some telephone contact was made in the most general terms. He mentioned the possibility of a substantial increase in room rates for the following year but the staff had dealt with this issue before and suggested they would get back to the conference officer with some ideas on rates later in the year. However the focus of the staff at that time was clearly on the production of next year's brochure and some new courses that they hoped to include in it. Eventually they phoned the conference officer again and suggested a meeting to talk about the approaching summer.

RESULT: They were told that since the conference officer had not heard from them or received any proposals he had offered all the beds and facilities at the college to a competitor for that summer.

2 Recruiting host families

How do you find suitable host families?

It is unlikely that you will be able to use your own accommodation staff at the year-round school to find families for a centre that could be anything from several hours to a flight away. One way round the problem is to appoint a local organizer or accommodation officer to act as your representative in the locality. Very often such a person is available through local contacts you already have but even if you know people who may be interested in the post it may still be prudent to advertise locally. Ideally your local organizer should have good contacts with local families and be willing and capable of providing the necessary degree of time and care required for the job.

The further involvement in the course by a local organizer in terms of booking centre and course facilities and arranging events will vary considerably from one organization to another but the local knowledge and contacts available through them should be utilized to the full. The rate for this type of role is usually based upon a set fee per student per week, a set fee per student or course or an overall set fee for the course.

The local organizer's role

Before the course

- Advertise for/find families
- Send out family questionnaires
- Inspect families
- Ensure families understand host family terms and conditions and sign agreement
- Provide headquarters with a host family register and necessary family details
- Place students with families
- Inform families about students' placement
- Book local facilities or events
- Arrange medical and other emergency health facilities
- Arrange airport transfers
- Provide families with copy of course programme
- Inform families of arrival and departure times
- Find staff accommodation

During the course

- Support course director
- Meet groups on arrival
- Meet group leaders
- Visit the centre regularly
- Deal with host family problems
- Deal with medical problems
- Deal with welfare problems
- Provide you with regular accounts
- Pay host families
- Arrange departure transfers
- Goodbyes to groups on departure

What information do you require from families? What information do families require from you?

The **host family questionnaire** will attempt to elicit this kind of information. It could look something like this:

Family Questionnaire				
Household residents				

Name	Age	Sex	Job	Interests
1				
2				
3				
4				

Address

Tel

Type of residence

No. of rooms

bathrooms

garden

pets

Number of beds/rooms available

Date available

References

Any relevant convictions

The **host family terms and conditions** would include information and conditions relating to the following:

Terms and conditions

- **accommodation**
  number of students
  number of students of any one nationality

- **bedroom**
  furniture
  change of bedding

- **heating**
  duration each day
  temperature
  source
  control
  (this is a source of minor problems in the UK)

- **use of:**
  bathroom
  kitchen and working equipment
  lounge
  telephone

- **laundry**

- **meals**
  packed lunch
  access to food and drink

- **security**
  front door key
  return time at night

- **arrivals**

- **departures**

- **daily travel** to and from school
  (show them the way on the first day)

- **expectations of the client**
  visits by group leaders
  hospitality
  welfare
  care

- **payment procedures**

- **damage**

- **insurance**

- **legal responsibilities**

- **what to do in the event of problems**

The **host family letter of agreement or contract** should include reference to:

- status of relationship or agreement between the school and family;
- the right to cancel on both sides;
- the rate of payment and how it is calculated;
- the host family terms and conditions document.

The **host family register** would include the following information:

- full names of all household members;
- address of household and telephone number;
- description of residence;
- summary of information on residents, eg ages, sexes, jobs, interests, smokers;
- information on pets.

3 Pricing a course

There are three basic factors involved in pricing a course:

- What are your costs?
- What do your competitors charge?
- What will the client pay?

How do you cost a course?

Fig. 7.1 on p 138 assumes twenty company personnel for a two-week residential technical training course including full board for twelve nights, twenty-four hours' tuition per week, specially designed materials, project-related visits, evening activities, one full-day sightseeing excursion and airport transfers. No particular currency is assumed.

How do you price a course?

Once you have a breakdown of direct costs per student or course you can move from this figure to a public price or fee for the course by looking at any indirect costs and other price factors (see Fig. 7.2 on p 139).

Indirect costs

You may wish to include some form of costing to take into account the indirect costs you incur from your headquarters, eg setting-up costs, travel to and from the centre to negotiate fees, administrative costs of registering and invoicing students, insurance costs, communication costs and distance management and quality control. Any evaluation of indirect costs will be, to some degree, subjective. In this particular example forty student weeks might represent 1 per cent of the total student weeks sold in a year. Supposing your total non-teaching overheads = 250000 per annum, then one way of calculating a reasonable level of cost would be to take 0.1 per cent of 250000 = 250.00.

Calculation of costs	Per student	per group(20)
Accommodation	**420.00**	**8400.00**
12 nights' full board at 35.00 per night = 420.00		
Classrooms	**108.00**	**2160.00**
3 classrooms x 24 hours per week x 2 weeks		
at 15.00 per hour = 2160.00		
Staff costs	**120.00**	**2400.00**
3 teachers at 400.00 per week x 2 weeks = 2400.00		
Materials	**50.00**	**1000.00**
Specialized in-house materials produced		
at a total cost of 1000.00 including labour		
Project visits	**30.00**	**600.00**
2 half-day project/visits		
Cost 2 coaches at 300.00 per coach = 600.00		
Evening activities	**37.25**	**745.00**
2 guest speakers at 100.00 per speaker		
Theatre visit at 15.00 x 23 people incl. staff		
Party at cost of 200 = 745.00 Total		
Excursions	**31.50**	**630.00**
1 coach at 400.00		
Entrance fees at 10.00 x 23 people = 230.00		
= 630.00 Total		
Staff expenses (x 2)	**83.25**	**1665.00**
13 nights' full board at 35.00 x 3 staff = 1365.00		
Travel to/from centre at 100.00 x 3 staff = 300.00		
= 1665.00 Total		
Transfers	**20.00**	**400.00**
Return transfer to centre from airport		
Contingency	**25.00**	**500.00**
To include 2 visits by a senior member of staff		
Total direct costs	**925.00**	**18 500.00**

Fig. 7.1: Costing a course

Profit margin

You may be looking for a definite percentage or no more than break even for a new project. You may be willing to cost in a very low margin of profitability if you are aiming for high volume take-up or a very significant unit profit margin if the scope of the course is limited in terms of numbers and the quality is high.

Government taxes

There are also government taxes of some form to take into account. It will depend on your local circumstances what level of taxation to include and whether you will be taxed on the net agent course fee (ie excluding any discount), on the gross public price or only on some aspects of your pricing. For the sake of simplicity, the example on p 139 contains a 20 per cent government tax on the all-inclusive fees less discount. This is by no means the correct or most effective manner to charge VAT in the UK where a number of options are available – see Chapter 5. This factor in pricing will depend on what government taxes apply and the manner in which you are permitted, or choose to apply them, will determine at what point and how you include them in your calculations.

Discount

Work out your pricing on the basis of the maximum discount you would be prepared to offer and remember all the other ways in which agents may achieve a higher real level of discount, such as free or discounted places for group leaders or students, free transfers or insurance. If you settle at less than this maximum figure you will be increasing your profit margin.

Continuing with the example on p 138, your aim is to arrive at a gross fee for the course:

Pricing calculation	Per student	per group (20)
Total direct costs	**925.00**	**18 500.00**
(See course costing) **Add indirect costs** (As analyses in the section on indirect costs above)	12.50	250.00
Sub total 1	**937.50**	**18 750.00**
Add 12% profit margin Sub total 1 = 88% of the fee you are now looking for so divide it by 88, multiply by 100 then calculate 12%	127.84	2556.82
Sub total 2	**1065.34**	**21 306.82**
Add government tax at 20% Sub total 2 = 80% of the fee you are now looking for so divide it by 80, multiply by 100 then calculate 20%	266.34	5326.71
Net selling fee to agent	**1331.68**	**26 633.53**
Add agent discount at 15% Net selling fee = 85% of gross fee you are looking for so divide by 85, multiply by 100 then calculate 15%	235.00	4700.03
Gross selling price	**1566.68**	**31 333.56**

Fig. 7.2: Gross fee calculation

How can you check your pricing?

Once all these factors are accounted for you have a provisional gross price you could publish and charge for the course. However there are several checks and balances you can apply to test out your hypothesis:

What is the worst scenario?

In calculating many of the direct costs you may have had to estimate numbers of students and class averages. Presumably this estimate is a cautious attempt to judge the minimum numbers you believe will attend the course given your market research in this area. Suppose you are wrong and owing to factors completely beyond your control you are well down on your estimated numbers. Just how low could your numbers be before you start losing money given the margin you have opted for per student? As part of this exercise you should also calculate exactly what your losses would be and what costs you would still incur if you had to cancel the course.

What price are your competitors charging for similar products?

Agents and clients are not going to opt for a more expensive course unless you clearly offer something more that they are prepared to pay for.

What will clients pay?

You have to consider the demand for your course and the upper limit your clients and agents would be prepared to pay. Can you increase prices or your margin by just a fraction and still retain your estimated levels of take-up?

4   Planning the course programme

What is a course programme?

PROGRAMME – WEEK 1							
	MON	TUES	WED	THURS	FRI	SAT	SUN
9.30	Testing & Induction	English Lesson	English Lesson	English Lesson	English Lesson	Full-day Excursion to London	Optional Excursion to Canterbury & Leeds Castle
11.00	Break	Break	Break	Break	Break		
11.15	English Lesson	English Lesson	English Lesson	English Lesson	English Lesson	or	or
12.45	Lunch	Lunch	Lunch	Lunch	Lunch	Sightseeing & Shopping	Treasure Trail and Crafts Workshop
2.00 ↓ 5.00	Swimming Tennis Basketball	Visit to Sea Life Centre	Mini-Olympics	Visit to Castle	Rounders Tennis Swimming		
6.30	Dinner	Dinner	Dinner	Dinner	Dinner	Dinner	Barbecue and Games
7.30	Party	Quiz	Ice-skating	Dancing Class	Disco	Film	

Fig. 7.3: A course programme

Planning a series of weekly programmes such as that above for a junior residential course is relatively simple once you know what sports, facilities and visits are within your weekly budget. In the case of an in-company course or ESP contract your programme would focus on the tuition in detail and any general course programme will probably need to be supplemented by a needs analysis, a syllabus, course timetable, specially designed materials and tests.

How do you book facilities?

Once you have a provisional programme for each week of the course you can begin to book the necessary facilities, visits and transport. You will find that certain facilities are not available when you have timetabled them and you will have to revise the programme a number of times before it can be finalized and fully developed to include more detailed information. Some of the bookings that will require further negotiation and checking as the course start date approaches include:

- number of beds or families per week;
- number of classrooms and hours of use per week;
- the use of a cafeteria and public relaxation areas;
- approximate numbers for meals;
- number of coaches, dates, destinations, etc;
- numbers for excursion or visit entrances;
- use of sports facilities – dates, times, numbers, etc;
- use of other rooms for evening activities, testing, office, etc;
- use of other facilities, eg library, photocopiers, videos, etc.

At this stage your bookings for facilities, rooms, visits, transport and events will still be provisional since you will be unable to guarantee final numbers of students. Very often the more established attractions and facilities will be willing to invoice you for the actual numbers attending on the day or only invoice you for facilities used. Most suppliers will appreciate your position and will be quite happy to adjust a provisional booking for your group as long as you agree a definite date by which you will finalize the booking. Clearly the closer this date is to your course start date the easier for you to be precise about numbers.

While you are adjusting provisional bookings you may also wish to address the following issues:

- installation of telephone/fax facilities;
- local banking facilities for the local organizer and course director;
- contract with a local taxi company for individual transfers;
- invoicing facilities with excursion and visit venues;
- book local performers and local events;
- find and book staff accommodation if this is not on-site.

Your correspondence and notes detailing your bookings for the programme will be essential information for your course director and knowing that he or she will inevitably have to re-arrange some events and bookings, you should also begin to compile a detailed telephone contact and address list of all suppliers and contacts for use by all your staff.

In the case of the larger more expensive bookings, such as classrooms and residential accommodation, you will have provisionally booked these on the basis of your original estimate of numbers but as the course date approaches you will need to revise your estimates up or down and keep colleges and residences fully informed of your latest forecast.

The importance of constant and regular communication and contact between you and the supplier, whether it be an expensive residential college, coach company or booking office for one or two tennis courts, cannot be stressed enough. The aim must be to pay only for what you use, reduce any penalty costs for not achieving numbers booked to a minimum, and ensure the maximum co-operation of suppliers to help you solve any problems with the course.

5 Managing classes and lessons

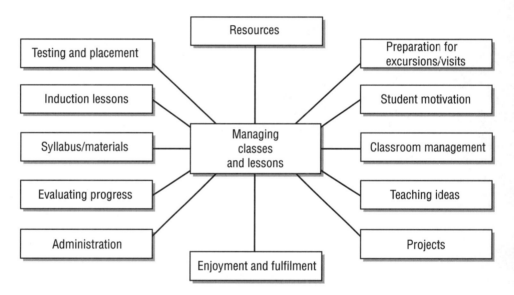

For the most part your approach to the management of classes and lessons with a contract ESP course or junior residential course will differ little from your management of year-round tuition and vice versa. The scale of adjustments required when managing various types of different year-round courses such as Cambridge Examination preparation courses and one-to-one courses are similar to those required when looking at the tuition element of short courses. In either case you have to take a variety of factors into account before determining an appropriate form of management for classes and lessons in a particular course.

What factors are involved?

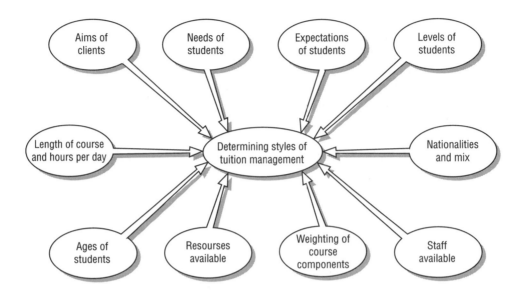

However, there are a number of areas within the field of tuition management in short courses which do require a slightly different approach from that used with year-round courses.

How do you test and place students on short courses?

Vacation students are usually on very short courses and the time you can allow for any form of testing and placement is minimal. For students staying less than a week you may only have a short fifteen-minute test to use as the basis of your placement. Even if they are staying several weeks you may be dealing with considerable numbers of students and the practicalities of the situation may demand that you use a short twenty-minute grammar and listening test in order to ensure that you are able to manage all the marking and placement on the same day. However difficult, a personal interview with the course director should always be included both as a form of placement and to ensure each student meets the on-site manager. On a day when you have continuing students and an intake of new students joining a roll-on roll-off course, time management of the process of testing, marking and placing will be crucial. How many old classes do you feed into and how many new classes do you form to ensure students are well placed with a minimum of disruption to everyone?

An ESP contract, on the other hand, may require you to include an in-depth needs analysis in addition to, or as part of, a very comprehensive and lengthy testing and placement process and this may include checking students' knowledge of specific areas as well as general English. Ideally, of course, this should have been carried out well before the arrival of the students.

In both cases you are unlikely to find a usable published placement test and some form of in-house test will probably have to be devised.

Although language level may be central to your placement criteria, there are other factors that may override traditional pedagogic policy:

- nationality, gender and age mix;
- relationships between subordinates and superiors within a group;
- relationships between friends or groups;
- filial relationships;
- length of stay and departure dates;
- numbers of students.

· ·

True story   *A day to remember*

The centre was large and well-established with an average of over 250 adult individuals at any one time. At the last minute a group of seventy requested to attend a short course at the centre. Although it proved difficult, the group were accommodated. On arrival they were tested and placed along with some other new students. Fearful of the effect on nationality balance in classes, the director of studies worked well into the night to ensure the group were distributed amongst as many classes as possible. When the group arrived the next morning to see what classes to attend they were very unhappy to find they had been split and some were to have morning classes while others were to have afternoon classes.

RESULT: A very tired director of studies had to change most of the classes on the first day and procedures were subsequently devised to ensure that group leaders are consulted before class placement takes place.

· ·

What should an induction lesson include?

Language work	Course information	Local information
Ice-breakers	Lesson/activity times	How to get home
Warmers	Aims of course	Shop/bank times
Classroom language	Activity programme	Where to go
Host family language	Books and materials	Where not to go
Example mini-lesson	Classroom and other rules	How to deal with problems
Useful questions	Programme for the day	Shoplifting/drinking
English money		Travel and transport
		Looking at the map
		Safety

The amount of information and language preparation will obviously depend on the time available. This may vary from forty-five minutes on a mini-stay course to a whole day or more on a contract ESP course. Even if the classroom induction lesson is very short, there may be more out-of-class time that can be devoted to a more practical induction in terms of local information.

The induction lesson is often the first real contact students have with staff and the success or otherwise of these lessons will have a considerable effect on students' initial attitudes to the course. There is no doubt that if students like the initial approach to language learning and have basic information about the course and locality, then they will feel more secure, more relaxed and you are more likely to get off to a good start.

At the beginning of a vacation course your staff may have only just arrived and been inducted themselves. Consequently it is useful to have planned and prepared induction lessons for the teachers. These may include detailed lesson plans for the inexperienced teacher or simple checklists and notes of the areas and points to cover for the more experienced members of staff.

How do you design and produce syllabuses and materials?

You may not be directly involved in choosing, designing and producing syllabuses and materials, but the teachers or director of studies you delegate these tasks to may have little experience of short courses or the needs and problems of short course students, and therefore your involvement at various levels of decision-making may be required:

- What are the realistic aims for the course?
- What specific needs and requirements do students have?
- Are there good published syllabuses and materials?
- How much will published materials cost?
- When will they have to be ordered?
- Do you have the necessary expertise and available time to design and produce syllabuses and in-house materials?
- What are the benefits and disadvantages of in-house materials?
- What are the total costs of producing in-house materials?
- How qualified and experienced will your teachers be?
- What supplementary materials can you provide?
- How will you package and distribute them to the centre?
- How do you deal with a roll-on roll-off course?

What other strategies, guidance and help can you give teachers?

One method of providing relatively inexperienced teachers with strategies and guidance in order to help them deal with some of the difficulties and issues they may face teaching on a short course is to produce a staff handbook containing ideas, recipes and advice for dealing with issues which may be particular to the short course:

Staff Handbook

Contents

Teaching

Monolingual classes or monolingual groups

Multilingual classes that include a high
    proportion of monolingual groups

Juniors and adolescents

Older students and the retired

Mixed level classes

Roll-on roll-off courses

Lessons

Teaching new language

Teaching from authentic/technical materials

Teaching technical vocabulary, skills and
    contextualizing learning

Motivation

Making learning enjoyable

Motivating unwilling students

Maintaining classroom discipline

Evaluating and demonstrating progress

Managing project work

Resources and Materials

The available materials and resources

Using the materials and resources

Exploiting the centre, locality and area in class

Preparing for excursions and visits in class

6   Managing activities and excursions at local centres

You may employ a team of activities organizers and a team leader, or in smaller centres you may require teachers to teach for half a day and organize and supervise activities for the rest of the day. In either case you will need to specify the role, functions and responsibilities involved in managing activities and excursions. See also Chapter 6, Section 7, pp 124–6.

How do you manage activities?

- Check activities bookings are confirmed.
- Check how entrance fees are to be paid.
- Check the venue is expecting the actual numbers.
- Produce a clear and interesting programme.
- Distribute a copy of the programme to everyone.
- Ensure everyone knows what they are doing, when and where.
- If possible, allow participants to choose their activities for each day.
- Check each student or group is present for each activity.
- Ensure staff and group leaders know their roles and functions.
- Divide students into manageable groups.
- Delegate someone to be responsible for each group.
- Provide variety and a choice of activities whenever possible.
- Always have a contingency plan or replacement activity.
- Aim for all activities to be well supervised, fun and challenging.

How do you manage excursions?

Many of the above points can be adapted equally well to the organization and supervision of excursions and visits but, inevitably, the problems of dealing with large numbers of juniors increase once you travel off-site and visit cities or large tourist attractions. Excursions are expensive and are often seen as the high points of a vacation course. As such they must be seen to be well organized, interesting and enjoyable. The following questions can be added to the list above:

- Check the coach is booked for the whole time you need it.
- Check the destination and times are known to the coach company.
- Do your research on the destination or venue.
- Use classroom time to prepare for an excursion or visit.
- Check everyone knows when and where to meet the coach.
- Lodge a list of those travelling with the local organizer.
- Check numbers carefully – don't leave anyone behind.
- Make sure groups know when and where to meet during the day.
- Be prepared for travel sickness and minor incidents.
- Inform families or catering staff if you will be returning late.
- Always organize the day – don't leave students to fend for themselves.

What makes a successful activities programme?

The success or not of your activity and excursion programme will depend on four basic factors:

- the personality, commitment, expertise and enthusiasm of your team;
- the degree to which it is organized and seen to be organized;
- the choice, variation and interest of the activities and excursions;
- your ability to meet the requests and changes clients will want.

In the same way that you need a balanced and varied teaching team, you need a balanced team for activities. Your ideal team may include serious amateur sports coaches, creative and innovative arts and projects enthusiasts, semi-professional tour guides, educationalists with expertise in certain topics and subjects, holiday camp redcoats and people with the ability to organize hundreds of students. In fact of course you will be seeking activity organizers who combine all these attributes. However you may be required to ensure that certain special needs are catered for by employing specialists or qualified staff.

Although you can book activities and excursions from head office before the course, you may only be providing a provisional framework which will be modified, added to and possibly rewritten once the course begins and the students and group leaders arrive. This may happen for a variety of reasons:

- your supplier may be unable to meet your bookings;
- your numbers may have changed;
- the weather may necessitate changes;
- group leaders or students may wish to change or rearrange events;
- your course director or activities team may wish to add other events;
- there may be a demand for additional activities and excursions.

Consequently you may have difficulty organizing the programme in detail and your role may be to provide a basic framework which the course director and activities organizers can build on. To help them in this task you can supply:

- a list of contact names, addresses and telephone numbers;
- necessary local information on facilities, attractions and events;
- provisional venue and transport bookings;
- a provisional programme;
- guidelines on how to produce a programme;
- ideas on how to distribute and 'sell' it;
- suggestions and ideas on how to organize activities and excursions.

The other side of the coin, however, is that you have marketed and sold a course and a provisional sample programme and therefore you have to ensure that students and clients feel they are getting what they have been sold and have paid for. You must be careful that the programme is not altered for the sake of it and that overall, the changes and modifications to the original programme enhance the course and meet the expectations of clients. Similarly, you have costed the programme carefully and although you will have a margin to play with on your costings, this can quickly disappear if the course director agrees to all the requests the clients and students will make. You must retain financial control of the programme and any changes should be approved before they are made.

How do you ensure adequate levels of supervision and safety?

Unlike the normal classroom situation, where you know where everyone is and your general employee and public liability insurances cover all eventualities, the situation can be much less certain once students start travelling and participating in sports and activities elsewhere. You must check that your suppliers have the necessary qualifications, licences, safety and health certificates, and insurances to perform the service you have sub-contracted from them. The degree of care, supervision and preparation required obviously increases when you are organizing and providing activities and visits direct. You must ensure you have met any legal, health, safety and insurance conditions required in order for you to offer the activity or service. At the extreme end of the scale you are responsible for a junior at any time throughout the course and you must know where they are, what they are doing and that they are being properly cared for and supervised by your staff at all times.

Students should be accompanied in ratio of one member of staff to twenty or thirty adults, one to ten juniors, depending on age, general behaviour and the opportunities for getting lost. For juniors especially, you need these three emergency procedures in place:

1 Meeting places/pickup times must be made clear, in writing, on a map if needed.
2 All students should carry an emergency school phone number and instructions on how to call it. The accompanier should give them clear guidelines on when to call and *exactly* what procedure to follow if they get lost or miss the bus. (This is not unusual!)
3 Identity cards should clearly identify the students, the school and how to make emergency contact. They should be clearly comprehensible even if the holder is a beginner in terms of language level, and unable to explain him- or herself to a local person or passer-by.

True story   *Every course director's nightmare*

The group decided to complete their course with an additional weekend trip to Edinburgh and asked the school to arrange the visit and supply a teacher to show them round the sights properly. The school staff booked the accommodation, sightseeing trips and transport. The coach departed with forty-seven students, four group leaders and a teacher. The weekend was a great success, apart from the weather. The teacher phoned to check confirmation of flight details since the coach was taking the group direct to Heathrow airport for their departure. With the usual chaos, farewells and luggage handling the coach departed from Edinburgh early on the Monday morning. Stopping in the north of England for a break, some students noticed two other students were missing. After several counts it was discovered there were forty-five students, four group leaders and one teacher on the coach. The teacher had believed the group leaders were responsible for head counting while the group leaders had presumed the teacher was.

RESULT: A certain amount of panic. The coach returned to Edinburgh and picked up the two students, who had overslept. The school contacted the airline and secured their agreement to hold the flight until the group arrived.

7 Quality control for short courses

The responsibility for quality control will rest with the member of staff managing the course or centre. This may be a course director or a director of studies, or in the case of a large course or centre you may have both.

Your decisions and choices of course director and director of studies for a centre will almost certainly be the most important you will make concerning your management of a short course. Taking the two roles together, the major areas of responsibility could include:

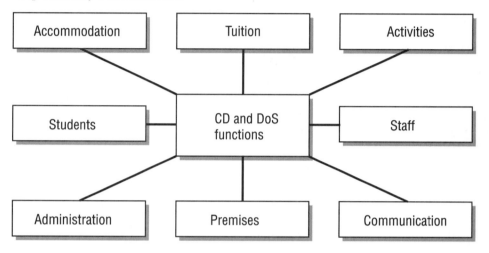

How do you ensure students are successfully accommodated?

Residential accommodation

- Check all the bedrooms and wash areas before the course starts.
- Ask the residence to make any necessary repairs, etc.
- Check security arrangements.
- Check standards of cleaning regularly.
- Check telephones, laundry and other services are operational.
- Place students with care and ensure their wishes are taken into account.
- Escort students to rooms and show them around.
- Check you know who is placed where at all times.
- Make sure students are aware of all available facilities.
- Implement a system for students to discuss problems with you.
- Make students fully aware of any rules of the residence.
- Ask students to keep the residence tidy.
- Ask for the accommodation feedback questionnaires to be returned by the middle of the course and act on them.

Host family accommodation

The responsibility for host families and students' relationship with them will almost certainly be a function of the local organizer for the centre. However, the local organizer's effectiveness will be seriously reduced unless you ensure group leaders, staff and students understand the local organizer's role and are encouraged to meet and discuss any queries and problems they may have. This entails informing everyone where and when the local organizer will be available at the centre.

How do you ensure students are taught well?

- Encourage an atmosphere in which classes are expected to be enjoyable.
- Require classes to start punctually.
- Provide teachers with useful information on classes and students.
- Discuss student needs, class needs and levels with teachers.
- Require teachers to plan weekly course teaching timetables.
- Support and help teachers when planning their courses.
- Appraise teachers.
- Check teachers understand the syllabus and how to use the materials.
- Provide a programme of in-service training and observation.
- Teach some classes and relieve teachers for peer observation.
- Train teachers to manage class feedback sessions effectively.
- Talk to group leaders and students about their classes.
- Discuss feedback with teachers, group leaders and students.
- Check classrooms are well equipped and laid out.
- Induct teachers in the use of any resources and hardware.

How do you ensure activities and excursions are successful?

- Produce an eye-catching programme and distribute it to everyone.
- Require the programme to be varied.
- Encourage students to make some suggestions.
- Modify the programme as requested, whenever appropriate.
- Encourage the activities team to 'sell' each activity/excursion.
- Brainstorm different ways to approach each activity with organizers.
- Require activities and excursions to be well prepared and organized.
- Involve group leaders whenever possible.
- Require activities and excursions to start punctually and finish on time.
- Ensure that activities and the planned itinerary for excursions happen, irrespective of the apparent mood of students on the day.
- Check all bookings carefully.
- Involve any and all staff whenever possible – including yourself!
- Make sure activities are challenging, varied and enjoyable.
- Provide the highest possible levels of care and supervision.

How do you ensure students are learning and enjoying themselves?

- Talk to students and encourage all staff to talk to students and spend time with them.
- Make sure they know your office is always open to them.
- Require classes to have regular short feedback sessions.
- Ask staff and group leaders to inform you of any student problems.
- Operate a suggestions box.
- Act and be seen to act upon mid-course feedback forms, requests, queries and complaints.
- Ensure students know what events and facilities are available for their use in their free time.

How do you ensure staff are performing at their best, developing and enjoying themselves?

- Be clear about their contract and what is expected of them.
- Clarify the aims of the course and how staff contribute to those aims.
- Induct staff properly.
- Inform them about all aspects of the course.
- Take an interest in what they do and support them.
- Give them clear feedback on their performance with time to act on it.
- Demonstrate that you value them and their contribution.
- Support and help any staff in positions of responsibility.
- Develop a team atmosphere.
- Explain your policy to clients, group leaders and visitors.
- Make sure they know your door is always open to them.
- Encourage them to let their hair down occasionally.

How do you ensure the course administration is effective?

- Check you know all the administrative procedures.
- Add to them where necessary.
- Check the staff know the administrative procedures.
- Explain why procedures are necessary and require them to be followed.
- Check head office has the administrative information it requires.
- Check you have all the necessary information for students, staff, the college, etc.
- Check staff are paid correctly.
- Keep your accounts up-to-date.
- Control expenditure and stay within budget.
- Manage student problems rapidly.
- Know where everyone is at all times.
- Deal with administration efficiently and unobtrusively.

How do you deal with premises and catering?

- Check premises before and during the course.
- Discuss problems, repairs and maintenance with the college.
- Exploit the relationship between the college and headquarters.
- Deal with and be seen to deal with damage and misbehaviour quickly.
- Tour the premises daily and check they are kept tidy.
- Eat with the students and encourage catering suggestions from them.
- Discuss catering arrangements, problems and requests with the catering staff regularly.
- Ask students, group leaders and your staff to deal with college and catering staff in a friendly and professional manner.
- Make sure students are aware of catering arrangements and any queuing and ticket systems in operation.

What is the secret of success?

Underlying the success or not of the course and your management of it will be the degree to which you have effectively built relationships and successfully communicated with everyone concerned:

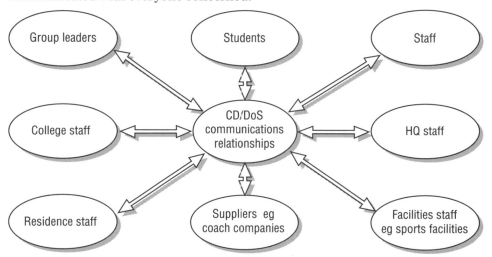

It is not enough to have a chat as you pass in a corridor or to only meet formally at scheduled meetings. All the possible forms of contact and communication must be used: one to one, telephone, fax, formal meetings, informal meetings, social occasions, notice boards, etc.

Obviously, some forms of communication are more appropriate than others, depending on who you are talking to and the point of talking to them. Most of your contact with headquarters, facilities staff and suppliers will be by telephone or possibly fax. Your communication with group leaders will involve formal and informal meetings, one to one and social contact. The timing of this contact and of formal meetings will make a real difference particularly at the beginning of a course. To gain full co-operation, help and support from all these different groups, you must provide as much information as possible, ask for suggestions and ideas, involve people in the finalization of the programme and act on their requests and concerns wherever possible.

What do you discuss?

Group leaders	Staff	HQ staff
Classes/lessons	Arrivals/departures	Arrivals/departures
Students	Students/classes	Transfers
Groups	Groups	Finance
Activities/excursions	Activities/excursions	Agent feedback
Accommodation	Teaching	Staff
Catering	Group leaders	Group leaders
Premises	Materials and resources	Accommodation
Group programme	Equipment	Premises
Group leader role	Administration	Materials and resources
Supervision/rules	Feedback	Feedback
Problems	Problems	Problems
Feedback	Supervision	Groups
Arrivals/departures	Premises	Management

College staff	Residence staff	Facilities staff/Suppliers
Arrivals/departures	Arrivals/departures	Numbers
Classrooms/rooms	Keys	Dates
Public areas	Bedrooms	Times
Activity events	Common rooms	Costs
Catering	Cleaning	Payment
Cleaning	Damage/misbehaviour	Equipment
Damage/misbehaviour	Maintenance	Supervision
Staff attitudes	Staff attitudes	Staff attitudes
Equipment	Security	Damage/misbehaviour
Maintenance	Supervision	Destinations
Supervision	Wash rooms	Activities
Other facilities	Other facilities	Problems

Students		
Welcome	Feedback	Change of class
Day 1 – Brief induction	Problems	Future courses
Who to see about what	Welfare	Special needs
Overview of the course	Questions	Goodbyes

• •

True story   *A great course in spite of ....*

The problems only became apparent once the course had started. The last-minute building works at the centre necessitated a change of classrooms. The cleaning of bedrooms was very poor. The centre was inadequately staffed. The activities programme had to be completely rearranged because the sports facilities had not been properly booked. The local organizer was taken ill in the second week of the course and the weather was appalling. It was with some trepidation that a trouble-shooter travelled to the centre each week to see the students and group leaders.

RESULT: The feedback was excellent, the problems dismissed as insignificant and the atmosphere was buzzing. The course director had communicated and involved everyone in the handling of each 'disaster' and the message that such problems, however serious, were not going to prevent everyone having a great course had been sold, taken on board and acted upon by everyone as a team.

8   Managing groups and group leaders

The management of groups of students and particularly younger learners is very much easier once a group leader is appointed and their role established. One way of ensuring you and group leaders agree on their role is to produce a group leaders' guide and use it as the basis of a discussion with them to agree what is expected of them.

Who are group leaders?

- the agent acting as a group leader for their group;
- office employees of an agent;
- friends or relatives of the agent;
- teachers with their classes from a school or college booking direct or through an agency;
- people recruited by the agent to be group leaders;
- senior members of the group of students;
- one of the students in a group;
- a member of your staff appointed by you to act as a leader.

Why does someone become a group leader?

- to provide an educational and cultural experience for their students;
- the salary or payment;
- the travel experience;
- a holiday;
- the cultural experience;
- the free place;
- to see relatives or friends;
- an interesting add-on to their job;
- as part of their teaching duties/interests;
- to take a teacher training course;
- to improve their language skills.

What roles can group leaders perform?

- full-blown teaching/activities assistant;
- activities organizer/assistant;
- supervisor of non-course/free time;
- accommodation liaison supervisor;
- team leader of group leader team;
- dispenser of course funds for additional activities;
- dispenser of pocket money;
- lunch and break-time supervisor;
- liaison officer between students and course director;
- head-counter and student discipline officer;
- general helper around the office and staffroom;
- trainee-teacher or student.

What do they get paid?

- commission;
- salary or wage;
- travel, expenses and costs;
- nothing;
- free course.

How important are they?

- If they are the agent then they will evaluate the course and decide whether they will continue to use you for other courses.
- If they are responsible for a group but have booked through an agency they will evaluate the course and decide whether to use that agency for further courses. The agency will in turn decide whether to continue selling your courses on the basis of their feedback.
- If they are a relative, a friend or an employee of the agent then the agent will take into consideration their evaluation of the course but may also be willing to listen to your evaluation of the group leader and the course, and the students' evaluation of the course.

How do you deal with group leaders?

- Regular communication at all levels is essential from day one.
- Provide them with all the information they need.
- Involve them in the planning and organization of the programme.
- Listen to their requests, suggestions and ideas and be seen to.
- Modify, change and meet their requests if you can or explain why you do things and why you don't meet requests.
- Treat them as clients.
- Ensure your staff and the centre staff treat them as clients.
- Build a relationship with them and ensure they enjoy themselves.
- Use their capabilities, availability and interest to the full.
- Talk them through your 'guidelines for group leaders' if appropriate.

• •

True story *Cinderella*

The group leader was a **nuisance**. Nothing was right for her – her students were in the wrong classes, the activity programme had to be altered daily, the excursions had to be rearranged and any student with a problem had to be moved immediately. She had a new special request every day. She was always late and was hopeless as an organizer or supervisor for activities. Then a week before the course finished a student had a serious accident and was admitted to hospital.

RESULT: The group leader never left the student's bedside and remained with the student for two weeks after the course had finished until the student was well enough to travel. The staff wondered what they would have done without her.

• •

9 Centre administration

What administrative functions are required from headquarters?

You will have to deal with clients, colleges, local organizers, suppliers and staff on a variety of issues across the spectrum of management sectors.

Education and operations

With clients
Centre programmes
Special quotations
Catering for special needs
Meetings at centres during the course

With colleges and residences
Finding and securing centre
Provisional and up-dated bookings
Regular contact

With local organizers
Induction
Host family terms and conditions
Host family rate
General support
Administrative back-up
Regular contact

With suppliers
Negotiations
Bookings

With course directors
Course programmes
Administration procedures
Resources, materials and equipment
Centre packs (see p 158)
Regular visits during the course
Induction and briefing
Details of all bookings
Centre programmes
Budgets and management decisions
Course directors' manual
Guide for teachers
Guide for activities organizers
Guide for group leaders
Daily contact and problem solving

Personnel

With local organizers
Recruitment
Contract and job description
Terms and conditions

With course directors
Recruitment
Contract and job description
Terms and conditions
Staff contracts and CVs

With staff
Recruitment and placement
Contract and job description
Terms and conditions

Marketing and sales

With clients
Brochures and publicity materials
Quotations
Negotiations
Visits to centres
Problem solving

With course directors
Information on group
Help and support with clients
Regular visits to centres
Liaison with clients about students

Registrations

With clients
Enquiries
Allocation of course places
Allocation of beds
Student bookings
Confirmation of bookings
Confirmation of accommodation
Invoices
Transfer arrangements
Course changes

With course directors
Student information
Numbers forecast
Arrivals and departures
Transfer arrangements

With colleges and residences
Numbers forecast
Arrivals and departures

Accounts

With clients
Payments and debt collecting
Discount statements

With local organizers
Local organizer payments
Family payments

With staff
Payment of salaries

With course directors
Process centre accounts
Provide access to cash
Invoicing facilities

With colleges and suppliers
Process and pay invoices

What to include in a centre pack

You can get some idea of the administrative procedures required at a course centre by listing the kind of administrative documents and other items you might send to a centre as part of the centre package:

Copies of test	Teacher handbook	Sports equipment
Marking templates	Activities handbook	Activities equipment
Blank class lists	Materials guide	Teaching aids
Registers	CD file/handbook	Cassette recorders
Teaching timetables	DoS handbook	Cassettes
Course timetables	Teaching materials	TV/videos
Student cards	Projects	Video cassettes
Luncheon vouchers	Excursion information	OHPs
Activity vouchers	Tourist information	Camera
Feedback forms	Teacher appraisal form	Teaching stationery
Reports	Teacher observation form	Teaching resources
Certificates	Group leader guide	First aid kit

For each item listed in the package there will probably need to be some formal or informal administrative procedure staff must know and use.

10   Managing the centre from a distance

The distance between the centre and your year-round staff and school will cause difficulties and there will be a time lag between the occurrence of events and your knowledge of them.

What can you do to compensate for distance?

- Make sure all the necessary planning is completed.
- Be clear to clients about what they are getting.
- Choose the right person as course director and director of studies and induct them properly.
- Give the course director and director of studies time to get to know the centre before the course starts.
- Provide the course director with all the information they require.
- Recruit good staff for the centre and induct properly before the course starts.
- Maintain daily/regular contact once the course starts – visit the centre and talk to everyone.
- Check that meetings are taking place.
- Require a weekly situation report that is brief but honest.
- Ensure your headquarters administration provides the necessary support and information.
- Respond rapidly to requests from the course director.
- Be prepared to troubleshoot on-site at short notice.

How can you ensure communication with the centre is effective?

You may phone your course director or be phoned by them several times during the day about practical issues and minor matters but you should not conclude from this communication that all is well. This contact may be no more than it purports to be and the greater issue of how the course is going may not have been touched upon.

You must both be aware that you are discussing the overall picture and addressing any potential issues that may have a negative influence on the course. Once this is clear you can ask for a snapshot of the course from the course director as it appears to him or her at that time. The course director will want to talk and you must ensure you listen carefully because as he or she is talking you must interpret this snapshot in terms of areas to focus on, what issues are worrying them most, what is not being said and what the general feel of the course is. You should take notes while the course director is talking and try to build a list of points to discuss further.

Having gained some insight into how you think the course is going you may wish to probe further, check your interpretation and revise it. You must then address the areas you both feel are in need of discussion. Your aim will be to provide real practical guidance on how to deal with problems once they have occurred and how to prevent potential areas of difficulty developing into problems. At the same time you will need to provide support, feedback, understanding and action where appropriate. You must also consider your course director as an employee and evaluate their level of stress and the effect this is having on the management of the course on-site.

When the course director puts the phone down he or she must be clear that you understand the situation at the centre and have been supportive, decisive and helpful where necessary. If you fail to ask the right questions and elicit the right information you may find it is too late to prevent difficulties and misunderstandings from snowballing and materially affecting the success of the course. However, telephone contact and written situation reports cannot replace face-to-face contact with the course director, staff and clients. The earlier you visit the centre the more likely you are to be able to identify, monitor and manage any potential areas of difficulty.

What can you do on-site to compensate for distance?

- Provide time for staff to get to know the centre before the course starts.
- Ensure the centre is well signposted and maps are available.
- Make plenty of use of the organization's name and logo around the centre and on all notice boards.
- Make sure rooms and public areas are laid out properly and do not look as if term has just finished.
- Personalize the centre – it is part of the organization but it is also distinct and needs an identity of its own.
- Encourage staff to personalize classrooms and use wall space where permitted.
- Keep headquarters well informed and use their expertise.

True story   *The truants*

The teenage son of an important politician and his friend were enrolled on a junior residential course in the north of England with the usual special requirement of careful supervision. With practised innocence they wove their web of deceit and convinced the course director that they were invited to attend an embassy party and stay the night at the embassy. The course director was by no means naïve but the boys were cunning and convincing. Being careful, the course director packed them off with a teacher who was driving to London for the weekend on the Saturday morning. As coincidence would have it, the boy's father, unable to contact the centre, called headquarters to request that his son be asked to phone him sometime that day. As soon as staff talked to the course director suspicions arose and a few checks quickly confirmed there was no party at the embassy and the boys were not expected there. At one stage the headquarters office had two international lines open to the father and the mother reassuring them, a line open to the junior centre seeking further information, lines open to other centres apprising them of the situation, an open line to the motorway police who had the description of the teacher's car and were trying to intercept it, a line open to the relatives of the teacher to try and determine where she might head for and lines following up friends of the teacher in London.

RESULT: Staff finally ascertained the teacher's destination. They contacted her on arrival, determined the whereabouts of the boys, put a London course director in a taxi to the location, 'apprehended' them and with a careful eye ensured they spoke to their parents and travelled back to their centre.

Typical traumas

(What would you do and what would you say if ...)

The course director calls in, you pick up the phone and ...

I am at the hospital, one of the students has had an accident horse-riding ...

We haven't got enough beds for all the arrivals on Sunday ...

One of my teachers has just resigned and I have no standby ...

The group are threatening to leave immediately – they say they were sold a campus course with all facilities on site ...

One of the group leaders is having an affair with our activities team leader ...

I've just had a call from the activities staff to say they have lost three students in Brighton – the coach has already been held up for an hour ...

A deputation of group leaders has just informed me that they think the activities are badly organized and boring ...

I've just had a call from the police – they are holding three students for shop lifting ...

One of my staff hit a student – it was only a tap but ...

I checked the disco was booked but when the group arrived they wouldn't let them in. By the time the organizer had argued with the management the coaches had disappeared. They have no transportation and are stuck in a rough area of London ...

The coach hasn't turned up, apparently it broke down. I have tried to find another coach but there are none available – we should have departed for London an hour ago ...

Some vandals got onto campus last night and caused trouble – the group leaders and students are worried about tonight ...

We had a flasher on campus last night ...

The conference office are furious – the fire alarm was set off three times last night, a snooker table was damaged, and ... and ...

The local organizer calls in, you pick up the phone and ...

One of my host family fathers has been accused of making an approach to a student ...

I have tried everything but I cannot place the remaining four students arriving this weekend ...

The group leader is insisting three students change families immediately even though they have only been here two days ...

This student has been moved twice but his present family want him moved tonight – I have no other family that will take him and I don't blame them either ...

I think you should know – some of the group leaders are complaining about the course director ...

11 Concluding remarks

Managing a vacation centre, ESP contract or in-company teaching team can provide more direct benefits than managing year-round courses. Usually the 'short course' will have a period of preparation and a clearly defined start and finish date. The rewards, challenge and satisfaction can be more than commensurate with the period of high pressure and workload on everyone's part to make it work.

Your choice of course director, director of studies and other on-site staff is critical to the success of the course, for even if the contract or vacation course operates within walking distance or adjacent to your year-round centre rather than many miles away, it is the centre staff that will implement your planning and deal with your clients direct. You can help, guide and troubleshoot from a distance but the day-to-day management and the successful provision of your teaching and other services will depend on your senior centre staff and their team.

You may find course directors and other senior staff to manage different centres or contracts over a considerable period of time but just because such posts are excellent training grounds for would-be ELT managers you may find such experienced staff often move on to longer term managerial positions. Consequently you will often be choosing a member of staff or applicant with a great deal of potential and interest but very little expertise in centre or contract management. In either case they will be working hard when the course or contract is running and will often be under considerable pressure. They will need your support, trust, advice and leadership. In return you will have to bring all your people skills to bear in your contact with them if they are to feel valued, understood and part of a team.

The traumas outlined in the preceding section give a flavour of how serious some of the issues you and the course director may have to manage during a course can be. Many of them can occur because of factors beyond your control and in spite of preparation and planning. In many cases the most you can do to prepare for this type of situation is to consider with your course director and other senior staff, as part of the induction process, what you might do if such issues were to arise. In fact, of course, your centre may, and probably will, run smoothly and successfully without the need to apply any such contingencies.

You may be unable to prevent many difficulties and problems but you can actively plan, prepare and manage the short course such that the students, group leaders, staff and centre managers all work together to make the course interesting, educationally rewarding and a thoroughly enjoyable experience.

Appendix   # Real-life samples and tasks

All the following samples are based on authentic data.

1   Marketing statistics

Here is an example of student statistics for a UK language school.

COURSE TYPE	Intensive general	Part-time (holiday)	1-1	Closed groups	Junior	TOTAL
YEAR/Quarter						
1990						
Jan-Mar	1098		19	50		1167
Apr-June	1244		45			1289
July-Sept	1392	956	45	60		2453
Oct-Dec	730		18	10		758
sub-total	**4464**	**956**	**127**	**120**		**5667**
1991						
Jan-Mar	780		10	12		802
Apr-June	949		39			988
July-Sept	1012	764	80			1856
Oct-Dec	992		19			1011
sub-total	**3733**	**764**	**148**	**12**		**4657**
% up/(down)	(16%)	(20%)	17%	(90%)		(18%)
1992						
Jan-Mar	743	80	15	36		874
Apr-June	633		12			645
July-Sept	783	749	40			1572
Oct-Dec	619		10			629
sub-total	**2778**	**829**	**77**	**36**		**3720**
% up/(down)	(26%)	8%	(48%)	200%		(20%)
1993						
Jan-Mar	621	381	5	28		1035
Apr-June	520	30	6			556
July-Sep	614	755	9	6	103	1487
Oct-Dec	635		12	12		659
sub-total	**2390**	**1166**	**32**	**46**	**103**	**3737**
% up/(down)	(14%)	41%	(58%)	28%		<1%

Units = student/weeks. One student/week is defined as 15 hours' tuition or more in 7 consecutive days. Junior course is for students 11-15 years. All other courses are 16+.

Task

How would you interpret the information on p 163? What trends are apparent? What implications might they have for strategy? Think about these questions:

- What is the school's main business?
- What is the long-term trend in that business?
- What is the main growth area?
- How has the school achieved that growth?
- What novelty has recently been introduced?
- How would you assess its success?
- What other trends can you determine?

Commentary ■ ■ ■

The school's main business is intensive general English. The long-term trend is clearly downwards; it is impossible to say whether this is because of things the school has been doing wrong (eg high price or poor promotion), or whether it is a general long-term trend. The first step here would be to decide this question by finding out whether other schools report a similar trend. In either case, the strength of the trend is very worrying: the school has lost 46 per cent of its main business in only four years, and has not made up that loss in other areas.

The main growth area is part-time and holiday courses, which after a dip are improving again. The school has achieved that growth by offering, and selling, those courses out of season – where they were formerly only 'third quarter' courses (ie summer only), the significant growth has been in the first quarter and to a much lesser extent in the second quarter. You could reasonably infer, accurately in this case, that this was the result of deliberate targeting of new geographical markets, as different nations and regions tend to have quite distinct and narrow holiday seasons.

The recent novelty is the introduction of a junior course. It is too early to say how successful it has been; you really need two or three years of consistent growth to be confident that a new course has really got off the ground. Although the junior course student/weeks amount to less than one-tenth of the part-time/holiday course numbers, it is not bad for a first attempt, given that a) the centre may only have been open four to six weeks in the summer, and b) the 'package' price may have been much higher than the adult courses.

Other trends:

1 the outlook for one-to-one courses looks bleak. This might be a reflection of the same underlying trend as for intensive general English; it might be that the school has deliberately run down, or at least not spent much to promote the one-to-one courses, as they are usually much less profitable, as well as less predictable, than group classes; or, as is probably the case here, it may be that many or most one-to-one courses are company-sponsored, and in times of recession companies trim their training budgets by cutting out non-essential language training or trading down from one-to-one to group courses.

2 Closed group courses appear to be on the way back up again, though still less than half their 1990 level. ■

2   Brochure text

Here are three samples, from real brochures, describing the content and/or method of a school's general English course for adults.

Sample 1

Language in action

The teaching method takes full advantage of the small group size. Students are encouraged to take part actively in class and not just sit passively taking notes from the teacher. New grammar and vocabulary are constantly practised in realistic situations, which students will meet socially or at work. Current events and social questions are discussed and topics from all aspects of modern life are tackled.

Sample 2

Aims
The object of our English courses is to promote the highest possible level of communicative competence. To this end, the principal focus is on the listening and speaking skills. Reading and writing are seen as essential tools in supporting this aim.

Programme
The syllabus is an eclectic one. Grammar, functions, language awareness, language appropriacy and pronunciation are woven together to create a wide-ranging and flexible programme. Each teacher is responsible for carrying out the aims of the programme by making use of teaching materials and techniques which combine a cognitive and creative approach to language learning. Textbooks, videos, cassettes, the teachers' own material and outside educational visits form the basis of the programme from which emerge activities such as grammar analysis, discussion and storytelling.

Sample 3

Method
Each class has two main teachers working closely together to ensure a balanced and systematic programme of study. One of them teaches mainly grammar and syntax and the other complements this with listening and reading comprehension, composition and oral practice.

Programme
Grammar: thorough systematic study of sentence structure, verb tenses, word structure, vocabulary.
Reading and listening: understanding and reproducing various styles of written and spoken English; different forms of oral expression.
Speaking: pronunciation, intonation and stress of English in different contexts; role-playing, reading of plays, dialogues and prose; conversation and discussion.
Writing: letters, reports, summaries, dialogues and compositions.

Task

Look at each of the samples on p 165 in turn.

1 Consider each one sentence by sentence and phrase by phrase, and try to put yourself in a potential student's shoes. What feeling or image does it evoke? Does it sound like the kind of programme you would want to follow in a foreign language? Why or why not?

2 How does the language of the sample read for a non-native speaker?

3 Which phrases do you like? Are there any phrases that set alarm bells ringing?

Commentary ■ ■ ■

Sample 1

It's good to exploit the small group size (maximum six students, in this case) here, as this is a positive feature that students pay for but may not appreciate the value of. Being 'encouraged to take part actively in class' is positive, although some students might feel threatened by not being able to 'just sit passively taking notes'. It actually mentions students and their real-life needs, which samples 2 and 3 don't at all! The word 'tackle' is perhaps too idiomatic. Overall, it's not innovative but it is short, simple and jargon-free.

Sample 2

It is a positive feature to state the aims, and refer to them in the 'programme' description, although this particular aim manages to be both blindingly obvious and jargon-based at the same time.

There is no mention of students in either section. The programme description in particular contains a lot of jargon. The more uncharitable might call it nonsense: 'woven together to create a wide-ranging and flexible programme'; 'combine a cognitive and creative approach'; a list of (unremarkable) educational resources 'form the basis of the programme from which emerge [*diverse but perfectly ordinary*] activities': did anyone think carefully about what is being said here?

'Eclectic' rings alarm bells: it sounds as though they make up the syllabus as they go along (full marks for honesty, but I wouldn't boast about it). 'Storytelling' is a valid fluency activity, but perhaps needs to be treated with caution in publicity material.

Sample 3

Most of us probably do have two teachers working on intensive courses, and it is a positive feature not just to say this but to explain that they work closely together while focusing on different areas (but what's the difference between grammar and syntax? – morphology? this is careless wording). I quite like the sub-skills approach of listing some of the contributory skills and activities, although the writing list is better than the speaking list. Does 'reading of plays, dialogues and prose' attract you? A 'thorough systematic study of sentence structure' might seem off-putting, more appropriate to a degree in linguistics than a language course.

In general, it's easy (and fun) to knock other schools' brochures. The three chosen here are in my opinion no better or worse than average (and they might well say the same about ours). These three seem to be mostly about the teachers or linguistic metalanguage (ie jargon). There is very little mention of the student, of his or her needs, in other words there is no YOU APPEAL: what will a course of study at this school do for YOU, the student? How will it build on what YOU bring to it?

The difficulty is to convey a clear idea of solid content and comprehensive structure while allowing the flexibility of customer orientation and responsiveness to individual requirements. You don't want to be prescriptive, and say the course will consist of X, Y and Z; nor do you want to say that the course content will be dictated solely by students' needs.

A related problem is that of length: words are precious pearls, particularly when you are writing for non-native speakers, but you need also to avoid going to the extreme of brevity of the brochure which begins with this introductory paragraph:

———————— WELCOME ————————

The school, which was founded in 1976, is situated opposite extensive municipal parks in the centre of [town]. We take pride in our high academic standards. Our school, which is small in size, is also noted for its informal intimacy created by our friendly staff. We occupy a three storey building with classrooms and a self-access centre, a student coffee room and a large patio at the back.

---

3   Booking terms and conditions

Introduction

The terms and conditions are the 'small print' in your brochure or on your booking form. In effect they set out the contract between the buyer (your student, agent or client) and the seller (the school). By completing an enrolment process where the terms and conditions have been made explicit, the buyer is deemed to have accepted those terms and conditions, and to have entered into the contract on that basis. Some schools actually make this explicit: 'Your application for a course and payment of a deposit, and our acceptance, constitute a contract,' or 'I hereby agree to accept the conditions of XXX School.'

Most of the conditions specify either a deposit or a time period/date by which something should be done (payment due date) or both. In some cases, you may wish to add a discretionary clause for refunds in exceptional circumstances but in general it is preferable to keep the terms and conditions as short, simple and explicit as possible; you can always exercise discretion in special cases anyway. As a rule, therefore, the terms and conditions tend to appear strict, unless you want to make a sales feature, for example, of an offer to refund outstanding course fees at any time.

Task

What might you want to do about the following issues?
How would you phrase the conditions in language that is simple and clear?

- **Deposit/enrolment fee**
  How much? When is it payable?
  What relation does it bear to the formal booking?
- **Payment date**
  When are the outstanding fees due?
  How hard should you try to get fees paid in advance?
- **Bank transfer charges**
  Where transfer of fees may result in the imposition of bank charges, who pays? The school or the student?
- **Increase of fees or variation of charges**
  Do you want to include a clause reserving the right to change fees or other details?
- **Cancellations and refunds**
  What is your stated policy on cancellations and requests for refunds of fees? How much of the fees will you refund and how much notice will you require?
- **Late arrival or early departure**
  What is your stated policy on refunds in cases of late arrival or early departure?
- **Insurance**
  Do you want to include a disclaimer of responsibility for loss or damage?
  What recommendation will you therefore make about insurance?
- **Insufficient numbers**
  What is your policy in the event of not having enough bookings to run a particular course? Do you want to mention it explicitly?
- **Behaviour**
  Do you want to say that you reserve the right to expel students for poor behaviour?
  What about their fees?
- **Public and school holidays**
  Will you make it explicit in the terms and conditions, or perhaps elsewhere in the brochure, that the school is closed on certain days?
- **VAT** (or equivalent local sales tax)
  Is it included in your prices? What allowance can you make for future variations in the tax rate over which you have no control?

Commentary ■ ■ ■

There are no right or wrong answers to the above questions. It depends on what conditions you want to set, and on local circumstances. What is vital is to ensure that the expression of your intentions is succinct and unambiguous. The authentic examples on pp 169–72 give you an idea of the range of policies that different schools adopt. They all come from the terms and conditions of UK language schools. Schools in non-native-speaker countries will obviously have terms and conditions in the local language that reflect local practice and legal requirements. However, the same areas will need to be covered, and it is well worth spending time collecting and scrutinizing the terms and conditions of as many local competitor schools as possible. You will almost certainly pick up some ideas for improving your own terms and conditions, perhaps in outline or in detail, or perhaps just making the wording more explicit or more friendly. If yours is already the best, you can feel justifiably smug!

Deposit/enrolment fee

'The School cannot reserve a place or accommodation until the Registration Deposit has been received.'
'The enrolment fee of £25 must be paid at the same time [*as you send in the enrolment form*] and is not returnable under any circumstances.'
'The deposit will be deducted from the fees for your course but will not under any circumstances be refunded once the enrolment has been confirmed by the college.'

Comment: Normally the deposit or enrolment fee is the expression of good intention that the school requires in order to confirm a booking. It is payable on booking and is non-returnable. A deposit is deducted from the outstanding fees, but an enrolment fee may not be (ie it is an extra charge on top of the tuition fee). It is usually a fixed amount (eg £25) but occasionally a deposit may be calculated as a percentage of the full course fee (eg 10 per cent).

Payment date

'All fees are payable in advance. To enable the school to complete all formalities in time, you are asked to pay your accounts at least one month before your course starts, earlier in cases of visa requirements.'
'All fees should be paid in advance, whenever possible.'
'Where fees have not been paid by the first day of the course, entrance may be denied.'
'If you enrol later than four weeks before your course starts all course fees are payable on enrolment. You may not attend classes unless payment or proof of payment has been received.'
'Please pay the balance of fees during the first week of your course.'

Comment: Most direct bookings will pay in advance, and in some cases can be encouraged to pay a considerable time in advance. Agents and companies may be less willing to do so, because for example they have their own contractual terms and conditions which specify payment halfway through the course or even after it has been completed and a satisfactory report delivered. The attitude 'These are our terms, take them or leave them. If you don't want our business, there are plenty of other schools who do' is not completely unknown. Restrictions on the transfer of money out of certain countries may affect the ability of their nationals to pay in advance. Payment in cash on arrival also avoids the school paying bank charges.

Bank transfer charges

'Please note the school is not responsible for bank charges.'
'[*For payment by bank transfer*] a bank transfer supplement of £5.00 **must** be added to cover UK bank charges.'
'Please note: we do not recommend Eurocheques or cheques drawn on banks in your country – bank charges on these are high and you will lose money. In all cases the school will expect to receive the full amount due in British pounds.'
'Students paying by Eurocheque may be asked to pay a surcharge to cover bank charges.'

Increase of fees or variation of charges

'The XXX Academy reserves the right to increase fees or charges without prior notice.'
'The school reserves the right to cancel or change the dates, times, fees or any other details relating to courses at our discretion.'

Cancellations and refunds

'Two weeks or more before the course begins: fees refunded (except deposit). Less than two weeks before course begins: 50 per cent refunded.'
'The fees for your course are payable in full in advance and will only be refunded in exceptional cases at the discretion of the Committee of Management.'
'Cancellations can only be accepted by letter or fax and the effective date of cancellation is the date the fax is sent or the date the letter is received. Cancellation with 28 days' notice – full refund less the £175 deposit and a £50 cancellation fee.
Cancellation between 14 and 28 days – 50% refund of fees less the £175 deposit paid. Cancellation with less than 14 days – no refund.'
'If you cannot attend the course (...) you should inform the School as soon as possible. You will pay only the deposit if we receive the cancellation before the course begins.'

You do need to spell your policy out, but this is probably the area where the greatest amount of discretion is needed in making individual decisions, as you have to balance purely financial decisions against the likely gain or loss of goodwill and future business.

Late arrival or early departure

'No refund can normally be made for late arrival, early departure or missing part of a course.'
'No refunds can be given except in the case of serious illness or accident.'
'Unused fees are refundable if you need to leave early for any reason.' (Makes a sales feature of this.)
'... long-term students who wish to interrupt their studies are required to give one week's notice to the School Secretary.'
'Once a course has started, refunds will be considered at the discretion of the School, but only in very special circumstances such as accident, serious illness or bereavement. In cases like this, the School will require written evidence of the reason for cancellation in order to consider a refund.'

Comment: One idea to bear in mind in the case of a cancellation or an early departure is the possibility of offering a credit note equivalent to the fees outstanding, less perhaps a fixed administrative charge. The credit is valid for a fixed period (eg one year) and is not usually transferable.

Insurance

'*[The school]* will not be held responsible in any way for any accident, loss or damage to students or their belongings howsoever arising during the course. Therefore, personal insurance cover is strongly recommended.'
'There is an insurance scheme for refund of fees in case of illness. This does not cost very much and students without this insurance will not get a refund of fees if they are unable to attend classes due to ill health.'
'Students should arrange their own health and personal belongings insurance before starting a course.'

Insufficient numbers

'We reserve the right not to run a particular course if the enrolment numbers are insufficient.'
'If as a result of unforeseen circumstances (eg an insufficient number of participants) a stay cannot be realized, we reserve the right to cancel it. The participant is advised of this and is given the choice of either transferring to another stay, or of being reimbursed money paid for the stay.'

Behaviour

'We reserve the right to ask a student to leave [*XXX School*] for persistent non-attendance or any serious misconduct.'
'Students whose behaviour proves prejudicial to the best interests of the School may be asked to leave before the end of the period for which they have enrolled. In such cases a refund will be made pro rata in respect of the period remaining.'
'The School can terminate a student's course at any time in the event of severe misconduct or disruptive behaviour, or if persistent absence or lateness continues after a warning has been given. In these circumstances fees will not be refunded.'

Public and school holidays

The School is closed on Saturdays and Sundays, and also on the following days: January 1–3 (New Year) (...) December 18–31 (Christmas).'
'The school is closed on public holidays and the last two weeks in December.'
'If a public holiday falls on a Monday, Course B begins on Tuesday and extra lessons are arranged to compensate.'

VAT

'All fees on this list include 17.5% VAT wherever applicable.'
'All fees include VAT at the standard Government rates. Unpaid fees are subject to a surcharge if the rate of VAT is increased.'

Comment: Most schools include all relevant taxes in the prices quoted, although in some circumstances companies (embassies, governments) can reclaim the tax element or are zero-rated, and it may be worth having a separate price list for them. A surcharge clause allows for a future tax increase, but the risk is that by suddenly asking for a surcharge you can alienate a client or agent who says, in effect, 'If your tax goes up, that's your business, not mine. Don't bring me your problems!' ∎

4 Analysis of fees

You have collected some examples of the fees charged by your competitor schools, and you want to make an analysis of them to see how they compare with yours. However, there are various differences, eg of course duration and number of hours per week, that make it impossible to compare them directly. How can you make a simple and quick analysis?

Sample

The general course

20 lessons per week for a minimum period of four weeks. Maximum class size 14 students.
Fees: 4 weeks £424   8 weeks £836   12 weeks £1250

The Cambridge course

Enrolment is for a period of 12 weeks. The Proficiency course is for 30 hours a week in a group of not more than 6 students. The Advanced and First Certificate courses are for 25 hours a week in a group of not more than 12 students.
Fees: Proficiency £1870   Advanced/First Certificate £1562

Vacation courses

20 lessons per week. Maximum class size 14 students. Fees include all excursions and social activities.
Fees: (Easter and Christmas) 2 weeks £242
(Summer) 4 weeks £504   6 weeks £750   8 weeks £984

Private lessons

per lesson of 50 minutes: 1 student £24   2 students £16 each

English for business

2 weeks of 30 lessons per week in a group of max 5 students £390

Task

Draw up a table with the following column headings:

column 1 = length of course in weeks
column 2 = number of hours/week
column 3 = total course hours (col. 1 times col. 2)
column 4 = total course price
column 5 = price per hour (col. 4 divided by col. 3)
column 6 = average group size (difficult: you may have to guess)
column 7 = income per hour (col. 5 times col. 6)

Using the basic information about length of course, number of hours/week and price, fill in the table for the courses you are interested in and comment on the analysis.

Column:	1	2	3 = 1x2	4	5 = 4/3	6	7 = 5x6
Course:	length in wks	hours/ week	total hours	price	price/ hour	av(max) gp size	income / hour
General cse 4 wks	4	20	80	424	5.30	*12*(14)	*63.60*
General cse 8 wks	8	20	160	836	5.22	*12*(14)	*62.70*
General cse 12 wks	12	20	240	1250	5.20	*12*(14)	*62.50*
Cambridge Prof	12	30	360	1870	5.19	*5* (6)	*25.95*
Cambridge Ad/FCE	12	25	300	1562	5.20	*10*(12)	*52.00*
Summer cse 4 wks	4	20	80	424*	5.30	*12*(14)	*63.60*
Easter/Xmas cse	2	20	40	202*	5.05	*12*(14)	*60.60*
Private lessons					24	1	24.00
Eng for business	2	30	60	390	6.50	*3* (5)	*19.50*

Notes:
1 The figures in italics are based on speculative assumptions.
2 The figures with an asterisk indicate an estimate of £20 per week deducted for the social programme.

Commentary ■ ■ ■

When comparing schools, there is the possible distortion effect of different non-deductible registration fees or charges for textbooks. If the sums are relatively small, it may be best to ignore them and accept that the results are crude, otherwise you may never get any usable information.

The comprehensiveness of analysis obviously depends on your requirements. If you are carrying out a marketing strategy formulation exercise or a major re-alignment of prices, then a full analysis is desirable, otherwise it is better to keep it as simple as possible.

It is often interesting as an academic exercise to see what discounts other schools give for longer stays, and to speculate about the reasons why some schools reduce much more than others. How many people get out their calculators and say to themselves, 'School X discounts 10 per cent over twelve weeks compared to only 8 per cent from School Y, therefore I will go to School X'? Probably not many, although in a highly competitive market, any price advantage could be significant. In the example above, the general course price for twelve weeks is only 10p per hour less than the price for four weeks – a discount of less than 2 per cent.

Where the average class size is not known, you have to estimate for this, so that the 'average' calculations for columns 6 and 7 are speculative. This is indicated by expressing column 6 as *12*(14) ('assuming an average of twelve students out of a maximum of fourteen'). For a thorough analysis, you can repeat the calculations using different assumptions of the class average – eg *7*(14), *10*(14), *12*(14) and *14*(14).

The figures in columns 6 and 7 are in italics to show that they are based on speculative group averages. The resulting data is therefore less reliable, but may well be revealing nonetheless. One of the striking features of the example above is that the price per hour (column 5) of all the general, examination and vacation courses is very similar, but that the income per hour (column 7) of the Proficiency course is half that of the others because of the small group size. This is surprising in view of the huge amount of extra preparation and marking work involved in teaching Proficiency. Did the people responsible for setting these prices do their own homework thoroughly?

The two most expensive courses, in terms of price per hour (column 5) – the private lessons and English for business – also have the lowest income per hour (column 7), again because of the small group sizes. This is where the class average figures become important. In determining your own pricing strategy, and whether it is even worth continuing to run such courses as high-prestige small-group business or executive courses, you need to review their profitability in the light of the historical class averages you have actually achieved, rather than the potential average or maximum occupancy rate. ∎

5   Adapting a course to meet a specific request

Task

Imagine your school offers a refresher course for non-native speaker English teachers. The course offers two weeks of intensive tuition covering teaching methodology and language improvement, the exact content and mix being determined by a questionnaire completed by course participants before the course begins. There are twenty-five lessons per week. The two-week course costs £400 for a maximum of ten participants. It is scheduled to run three times a year, in the current year 4th–15th January, 12th–23rd July and 16th–27th August.

You receive the following letter. How do you respond?

Dear Sir/Madam

We are a group of five teachers who are interested in your teachers' refresher course but would like to have a tailor-made course, if possible, including literature, history or English for business.

We will be able to attend the course starting on July 5th until 16th (twenty hours per week). Please will you send us all the information about fees as soon as possible.

Yours faithfully

A Tressera

Commentary ■ ■ ■

You already offer what the clients are looking for, therefore it is in your main line of business (the usual pithy management advice here is 'stick to the knitting'). There are, however, some significant differences:

- They are asking for specific dates which overlap but do not coincide with your published course dates.
- There is a maximum of five participants in their group, which will make a tailor-made course expensive, especially for teachers paying for themselves.
- They are asking for twenty lessons a week rather than your usual programme of twenty-five.
- They are asking for specific contents not included in your usual programme.

The three possible responses are:

1 to construct a course to meet their requirements exactly as requested; this is likely to be expensive;

2 to say 'No, I'm afraid we can offer you the scheduled courses only';

3 to propose a compromise between what they are asking for and what you already offer, with some flexibility built in, but you don't want to negotiate over every little detail. It's not worth it. You can, of course, offer a choice of **1** or **3**.

Looking at these options one by one:

Option 1

The tailor-made course will be expensive, as there will only be five participants. Supposing your average take-up of the teachers' refresher course is seven or eight out of a maximum group size of ten, then your average income from such a course will be £3,000 (£400 times 7.5). If you want to maintain this level of income, then the cost for each individual in a group of five is going to be £600. For two weeks of twenty lessons, this costs each individual 600/40 = £15 per lesson – almost double the scheduled course fee of £400/50 = £8 per lesson per participant.

This assumes that it costs you as much to provide a teacher for two weeks of twenty lessons as it does two weeks of twenty-five lessons, which if your training staff are on a permanent contract, is probably true. It does not take account of the extra time taken to prepare material on the specific topics mentioned nor of any staff scheduling problems of having two teacher-training courses overlapping but not coinciding.

Option 2

A few minutes' reflection, some quick calculations, a dash of intuition and as much experience as you can draw on may suggest that the chances of getting this business at a profitable price are just not worth the bother of a full costing exercise and a detailed reply – don't be a 'busy fool'! Send back the standard information about the teachers' refresher course with a covering letter saying you're sorry, you can't meet their specific requirements, but would they like to consider your scheduled course, details enclosed.

Option 3

This depends on which of the specific requirements you can most easily meet and which are the most difficult to accommodate. Some possible areas of compromise are:

- If you would really like them to join the scheduled teachers' course in some form, offer it at a special price **either** for the group of five as it stands; **or** with a nominal reduction for attending only four lessons per day rather than five; **or** with an extra 'closed group' lesson per day for the five of them focusing on one of the requested specific topics.
- You can offer observation of experienced teachers with your other classes as an optional extra bonus.
- If staff availability and the overlapping dates are the problem, offer a closed course based on dates a week earlier than those requested, so that your training staff can teach both the closed course and the scheduled one 'back-to-back' (ie one immediately after the other). ■

6   Analyzing a proposal from an agency

Task

Read the letter and contract conditions from the ABC Travel Press Inc. Imagine that your school has very few students from that country, and would like more: you need to decide whether their offer is worth serious consideration for your marketing plan for next year. Use this information as a basis:

1 Your average course price is $1000.
2 Your normal commission for agencies is 15 per cent of tuition fees.
3 You have a total advertising budget of around $25000.

Dear Sir/Madam,

I'm writing to you today because I have a proposal which will be beneficial to us both. It will benefit you by gaining greater school recognition, and more students.

As you probably know, ABC Travel Press Inc. is a highly respected publishing firm specialising in the 'internationalisation of education' field. We publish a variety of study abroad guides. Plus, with ABC's well-known and well-established overseas study abroad advisory centre, which counsels over 6000 students a year, it is common for students here to think of ABC when they think of studying overseas.

The proposal entails a combination of advertising and commission from your school + advertising and selling by our ABC staff. More specifically, we will promote your school in exchange for commission and placing advertising. By promoting, we mean placing advertising ourselves in our other publications, and 'steering' our students to enter your school. This we feel will get your school a better response than using agents alone, or advertising alone.

Please take some time to consider this proposal. I'm looking forward to hearing from you soon. Thank you for your time, co-operation and attention.
Regards

D Brown

International Marketing Division Manager
ABC Travel Press

Contract conditions

Requirement of the school

A. Placing of advertising

Minimum placement of two 1/2 page b/w advertisements per year (one term) or one full page in any of our publications. The price of the 1/2 page b/w advertisements will be US$400 each insertion, or US$800 for a full page insertion (if a contract is made for two or more years, the advertising costs will be US$350 or US$700 each insertion respectively). ABC Travel Press requires complete camera-ready artwork for advertising. If production is needed, ABC can produce artwork at US$100 for a 1/2 page, US$150 for a full page. Production includes layout and translation.

B. Commission

Each student will apply directly to your school. A payment of 15 per cent of the total amount of tuition should be paid to ABC Travel Press for each student which applies and enrols in your school with an application form which has an ABC stamp imprinted on it. Thirty days after the date of enrolment, a copy of each student's application form and the commission payment of a check/money order or bank transfer in US dollars shall be sent to ABC Travel Press. ABC Travel Press is not responsible for any cancellation of students after enrolment. Thus no refund of commission will be given.

Requirement of ABC Travel Press

A. Additional advertising/editorial

One full page editorial per year in ABC's English Institutes of the World Guide. One 1/4 page advertisement per year in ABC's Study Abroad Guide to ESL Programs.

B. Selling your institution to students

Recommending your school for enrolments. Giving pamphlets and brochures and showing videos of your school to potential students. Every two weeks, doing follow-ups on each prospect, checking for decisions, and providing more help to speed up the decision process. Assistance in filling out application forms and helping set up travel arrangements and insurance plans.

Commentary ■ ■ ■

- If you want more business from this region/country, you have probably already started to develop a marketing plan. Does this approach fit broadly with that plan?
- It's money upfront: although the contract does not explicitly say so, ABC will probably be asking for full payment of the advertising fee before or on the date of publication. That means a minimum of US$800, probably plus production costs, long before you're likely to see any return in terms of students paying fees.
- Note that the commission is payable thirty days after enrolment, irrespective of when the money is received by you. This might well mean that if a student enrols early, you will have to pay the commission to ABC some time before you receive any payment from the student.

- The clause about no refund of commission on cancellation is a bit tough, but it is unlikely to happen very often. If it does happen more than once or twice, it would be worth taking up with ABC immediately on the grounds that it might be in part the result of inappropriate counselling ('steering') by their staff.
- If you decide the proposal is worth serious consideration, you should get hold of copies of their study abroad guides. It would be entirely reasonable to ask ABC for sample copies, and to ask for the following information:
  1 How many other advertisers will there be (ie is it all adverts and no text)?
  2 Is there any limit on the number of advertisers from your area/region, or who are offering courses in your particular line of business?
  3 What is the print run of each guide? How many are distributed, to whom, by what means?
  4 Can they give any indication of the typical response rate to advertisements?
- You also need more detail about student numbers. It's not enough to say they counsel 'over 6000 students a year'. Of those, how many do actually study abroad with one of the schools they are promoting? Can they give some references of other schools they work with who will vouch for the viability of the scheme? Obviously, no one can give you any guarantees, but before you pay $1000 upfront plus commission, you are going to want some more solid information to go on.
- What is the word 'on the street'? Contact other advertisers and ask about results. This is where having good informal relations with other schools is very valuable – a five-minute phone call here could help you avoid a very expensive mistake. Speak to some other students from this country – have they heard of ABC Travel Press or their guides? Show them some samples: what do they think?
- ABC will need your pamphlets/brochures for distribution. How many? How do they decide who to give them to? How many brochures do they give to each individual enquirer? You do want them to give out your brochure, clearly, but only to people who have a reasonable chance of booking. Otherwise, it will be an expensive waste of paper.
- On the basis of the information given here, ABC appear to know their business, which is publishing information and advertising guides. But they don't make travel arrangements for students – what exactly does 'helping set up' mean? Do they just refer them to a travel agency down the road? Is this going to inhibit students from booking through them, as opposed to going to another agency who actually make the travel arrangements for them?
- If your standard rate of commission for agencies is 15 per cent anyway, you are going to pay ABC that much *plus* the advertising fee, so any students generated will bring you a lower net income than usual. How low are you prepared for this to go? How many extra students will you need to make this scheme pay?
- Let us suppose that on other exceptional occasions, you have agreed a commission rate of 20 per cent, and regard this as an absolute maximum, worth paying to get extra new business. The extra 5 per cent of commission costs you 5 per cent of $1000 (your typical course price) = $50 per student. So, the minimum advertising fee of $800 to ABC is the equivalent of paying an extra 5 per cent commission on 800/50 = sixteen students booking an average course. Therefore you might want to set an arbitrary figure of 20 extra students as the absolute minimum threshold for this scheme in the first year, with perhaps forty or fifty students as a target for success (spread over fifty

students, the advertising fee would be equivalent to an extra $16 or 1.6 per cent commission on top of the usual 15 per cent).

- Ultimately, you will only find out if it works by trying it – the iced lollipop test of 'suck it and see'. You can make it plain that you are giving it a trial period and expect the results to more than outweigh the costs by the end of first year in order to reconsider it in the future. ■

7 An example of external validation criteria: the British Council accreditation system

This section contains a brief outline of one external evaluation system. The British Council operates a voluntary inspection and recognition scheme for private English language schools in the UK (and a parallel validation scheme for state sector colleges). It is not being presented here as the ideal model for good practice, but the current system has been under continuous development since 1982, and was itself then based on earlier inspection schemes. It is therefore a well-developed scheme which undertakes around 100 inspections a year, mostly to the satisfaction of the schools who are paying for it.

There is a scheme handbook, known familiarly as the Red Book, which is readily available (British Council 1991) and describes the scheme and the recognition criteria in some detail. You might like to get a copy of the handbook and use it as a checklist for your own evaluation criteria or to construct a framework for self-assessment.

Here are some of the key features of the scheme:

- Two external inspectors visit each school every three years.
- A considerable amount of the paperwork is submitted to the scheme administration and to the inspectors in advance, so that when the inspectors come, they are looking at the daily operation, not shuffling papers. The documents submitted must include a full set of promotional materials.
- The inspection lasts one or two days, depending on the size of the school.
- The inspection should be timed to take place when a school is substantially full:

4.3.3 (...) At the time of inspection, schools must be able to offer a reasonable percentage of their maximum capacity of students, and an appropriate range, eg junior students if junior classes are a significant area of their intake.

The inspectors look at seven specific categories or areas of operation: management and administration, academic management, teaching, welfare, professional qualifications, premises, resources.

There are detailed criteria for each of these categories (about eighty paragraphs over eight pages altogether). Here are a few examples:

1 From the management and administration section:

5.1.1 The involvement of the owners in the daily running of the organization should be clear, and the degree of any delegation of control to appointed managers, should be well established and understood.

5.1.7 Staff contracts should be available for scrutiny, and should provide such reasonable terms for length of notice, holiday entitlement, sick pay, contact hours, lesson breaks and grievance procedures as may contribute to the effective and efficient operation of the school.

5.1.12 All ancillary services offered in publicity materials should actually be provided.

2 From the academic management section:

5.5.1.1 **Management of the teaching team***: special attention will be paid to the resources provided for teacher induction, monitoring, training and general support; teacher responsibilities should be clearly specified and supervised; adequate channels of communication should be maintained among teachers themselves, between teachers and the academic manager or director of studies, and between teachers and senior management (...)*

5.5.1.2 Course specification: appropriate objectives and syllabus content should be established for all courses; appropriate materials and methodology should be identified to achieve the objectives; there should be evidence of course development as appropriate (...)

In the teaching section, the inspectors observe every member of staff who is teaching at the time of the inspection, but not necessarily for a full lesson – maybe only twenty or thirty minutes each.

The section on professional qualifications spells out in some detail the requirements for teaching staff. At the end of the inspection, the inspectors give a 'de-briefing' in which they summarize their impressions, but without saying what grades or result they will recommend. The inspectors make their judgement on a snapshot view; in other words, they base it on what they actually see, not on what they think the school might be capable of. They subsequently write a report which is considered by a large committee on which various bodies and interests are represented; it is this committee which passes or fails a school. Where there are faults that are serious but rectifiable, this Recognition Advisory Committee may withhold recognition ('deferment') for a certain period, pending re-inspection, rather than failing a school outright.

The inspectors award a grade from A (excellent) to E (unacceptable) in each category:

4.4.10 In order to be considered for recognition, the organization will normally be expected to obtain <u>as a minimum</u>: a C grade in teaching; at least four grades of C or above; no grade of E (...)

The inspectors' task is to measure the school not against a single, imaginary, code of good practice but against the aims it sets itself:

4.4.1 Inspectors will assess the work which an organization is doing in pursuit of its declared aims. They will express an overall professional view of the organization and the way in which it is or is not achieving those aims (...)

and against the claims it makes for itself:

4.4.3 Additionally, the inspectors will verify the claims made by the organization in its own prospectus and other publicity.

They therefore look particularly closely at the school's promotional materials and want to see that it lives up, in spirit and in letter, to the claims it makes.

Over the years, all the criteria, and indeed the scheme as a whole, have been argued over time and time again, and are subject to a process of continuing debate and review and, one hopes, improvement. The important point is that the scheme strives to strike a reasonable compromise between allowing for a full diversity of valid organizational aims, on the one hand, while offering inspectors sufficiently specific criteria for them to be able to say, for example: 'Yes, what I have seen satisfactorily meets criteria X and Y, but doesn't quite meet criterion Z.'

References

British Council, 1991 *English Language Schools Recognition Scheme Handbook* Accreditation Unit, English Language Division, The British Council, Medlock Street, Manchester M15 4AA

Cameron, M., Rushton, A. and Carson, D 1988 *Marketing* (Penguin)

Charles, D. 1993 The Fronted Organigram: putting management in its rightful place. In *ELT Management*, Newsletter of the International Association of Teachers of English as a Foreign Language: Management Special Interest Group 12 (June), pp 11–15

Dibb, S., Simkin, L., Pride, W. and Ferrall, O.C. 1991 *Marketing* (Houghton Mifflin)

Handy, C. 1989 *The Age of Unreason* (Hutchinson)

Harvey-Jones, J. 1988 *Making It Happen* (Fontana)

Hoyle, E. 1975 Professionality, Professionalism and Control in Teaching. In Houghton, V. et. al. (eds.) *Management in Education* Vol. 1 (Ward Lock)

Hussey, J. (ed.) 1991 *Understanding Business and Finance* (DP Publications)

Phillips, M. and Rasberry, S. 1986 *Marketing Without Advertising* (Nolo Press, Berkeley, California)

Index